Children's Bedtime Stories

Fantastic and Short Stories That Are Ideal for Bedtime

Brenda Turner

A Palm Tree

Once upon a time, there was a palm tree, although it was not a particularly attractive palm tree. The tree's trunk was slender and spindly, and if the wind blows strongly, the tree will bend over, so the leaves at the top of its trunk were nearly scraping the bottom.

The palm tree resided in a little bay, a rugged bay with little sand on the shore. There were large rocks everywhere, as well as several little sharp rocks that sliced people's feet.

Too few tourists came to such an unappealing cover, and the palm tree was lonely.

The water didn't even come close to entering the harbor.

The sea told the palm tree, "I'm not going in there." It's just tiny and rocky and uninteresting.

Oh, please, the palm tree pleaded. Just come in and tickle my foot with your waves, much as you do in the other bays.

The sea didn't even try to react, instead of sweeping its tide even farther away from the beach and the small palm tree.

The tiny palm tree's leaves hang sadly down, and its little trunk bowed in disappointment. The large black rocks stood arrogantly around the tiny tree, as they often did, and the little rocks brushed against each other, sharpening their edges in preparation for cutting more bathers' feet.

And it would have remained that way if it hadn't been for Mr. Mistral.

Mr. Mistral was a powerful wind. However, unlike some heavy winds, such as Mr. Gale and Mr. Tempest. Mr. Mistral was a nice, kind breeze that was interested in what it was flowing against.

What the hell is going on? Mr. Mistral could see the little palm tree was angry.

It quietly listened to the little palm tree's cries for help for ten minutes.

Mr. Mistral could blast hard enough to uproot the little palm tree and sweep it into another, much better bay, but when it searched, all the other bays were full of palm trees, and there was no room anywhere.

The wind circled the little bay repeatedly, hoping to come up with something to cheer up the tiny palm tree. The wind became aware of something odd occurring the third time it approached the small oak. The more the wind remained in the rugged little bay with the little sea in it, the more wretched it seemed.

This place needs to be cheered up! It sobbed. For all these rocks and no shore, it's no surprise that everybody is unhappy here!

The wind then blew in a close circle around its mouth. Oh, my God! The large sand piles on the other side of the island whirled into the air, forming huge yellow clouds that raced across the island to the small rocky bay.

The wind then opened its mouth wide and sucked in a massive suck. The sand clouds came to a halt over the rugged bay, and because the wind had died, they dropped from the sky, filling the little bay with sand.

Unfortunately, the little palm tree was still covered; in reality, it was so well covered that only one little palm leaf poked out of the deep sand to guide the wind to where it could be rescued.

The wind gently whipped a breeze through the little palm tree, and the palm tree popped back up, amazed at the change the sand had created to the little bay.

The hideous black rocks had been hidden, and sharp rocks had been buried so deeply in the sand that they would never cut anyone's foot again. The bay had brightened up.

The shore, which peered around the corner of the small cove, was unimpressed.

It gurgled, "All my beaches have sand." That's nothing new.

While Mr. Mistral's rough blowing, the water failed to wash into the harbor, and although the tiny palm tree was not as miserable as it had been, it would have loved to have had its roots tickled by the ocean.

I'll send it a fair blow tomorrow and scatter some flower seeds from nearby gardens. Mr. Mistral spoke in hushed tones. They'll take a few days to rise, but they'll brighten up the room. But that's what I can do. Mr. Mistral disappeared over the horizon in a final whirl.

But the rain had sensed the wind speaks to the little palm tree, and the following day, as the little palm tree awoke, the rain patted the leaves of the little palm tree.

The rain gushed if you had water in your little port. I'm sure I'll be able to fill it!

The little tree was thrilled because for the next three days, it rained, and it rained in the little bay, and the bay quickly filled with water, and when the rain stopped, the sun came out, and guess what? The water sparkled and shone in the sunshine, and the wind returned with a soft breeze, causing the fresh flowers to wave and the tree to rustle a calming tune.

The tiny palm tree was overjoyed because if it had performed a somersault out of joy, it would have. But since trees are planted in the earth and cannot jump, the little palm tree simply swayed in joy.

The little bay had been the best in the region, and with all the goodness from the sand and water, the little palm tree developed and grew, its trunk being strong and its branches stretching out, providing shade with its fresh green leaves.

A couple of days later, the sea was going by the little bay as the normal, nose in the breeze, completely avoiding it, when a passing bird exclaimed, the sea in that little bay is much clearer than your sea out here.

The sea came to a halt; there was no water in the little bay; what was the bird worried about? As a result, the sea turned about and peered into the little harbor. It would have if the sea had hair that might stand on end in surprise. Although, as we all know, the sea has no hair, so it couldn't. Instead, the sea drifted in awe.

The bay had to be the greatest it had ever been!

It attempted to reach into the bay when it got near, but it couldn't.

Who is squeezing my water? A lovely palm tree was calling out to the water.

The water gaped as two waves smacked together.

It was the teeny-tiny palm tree!

But now, it was tall and slender, waving its leaves in a rather enticing manner. The sea falls in love with the palm tree right away.

Let me in, the sea sloshed. Since I adore you, I want to lick you and tickle your roots!

For a brief second, the palm tree grew brown with embarrassment; no one had ever cherished her.

She rustled, "I can't allow you in." Rainwater has accumulated in the harbor.

I will assist! It was a massive voice, the most powerful voice there is. But it wasn't a poor voice; it was a pleasant one.

I may steam the water up, allowing the sea to enter the small bay.

The sea and the palm tree both gazed up at the light, which was beaming back at them.

Within a day, the sun had warmed up over the small harbor, and the rainwater had evaporated.

The water came in with a thunderous clap; its waves reached out to the palm tree.

The palm tree swayed back in delight; this was the best it could be!

Soon after, the sea and the palm tree married, and HALLELULA! Two months later, the palm tree produced five large coconuts, which grew into five baby palm trees, who lived happily ever after in the lovely little bay with their mother and the shore.

The Good Health Fairy

Have you ever asked that certain people get sick and others do not?

I know why, but it's a huge mystery that I don't think I'm supposed to reveal.

You see, if I tell you, you'll tell someone else, and if everyone learns the trick, the fairies won't come.

No, no!

I should not have brought up fairies!

Excuse me as I stomp on my foot for being a jerk.

So, now that you've learned about fairies, I'll tell you why certain people are sick and others aren't, as long as you vow not to tell anybody, not even your thumb!

Do you have a promise?

Okay.

So I'll explain that certain people get ill and others don't.

Can you get that you sleep at night?

Isn't that that you're tired?

But do you remember that you're exhausted?

Since you've spent the whole day playing, working, climbing, and jumping.

Although something amazing happens as you shut your eyes and fall asleep.

The fairies have flown into your home.

It's pointless to say you've never seen them because you can't see them when you're sleeping.

The fairies have arrived to replenish all of the energy pots that you depleted throughout the day.

They enter through your mouth and begin dipping their little sticks into your little energy pots to see if they need more energy.

For example, you can have an energy pot for your mouth. Every time you talk, you are lubricating your tongue and allowing it to function properly. So whether you speak or weep a lot through the day, your mouth pot would be virtually empty before the fairy comes to dip it at night. Then the fairy would take her energy kettle and refill your mouth pot so you can chat the next day again.

You have energy pots all over your body, from your head, spine, shoulders, and limbs, as well as any other part of your body, even down to your toes!

So, what causes certain individuals to get ill when others do not? It all comes down to what people eat and drink. Those who consume healthier foods and drink nutritious beverages have far fewer health issues than those who eat a lot of sugar and greasy food and drink a lot of beer and wine.

Consider what happens as the fairy returns to replenish the energy pots of someone who has consumed an abundance of cookies and chocolates. The unfortunate fairy is coated with sticky sugar everywhere she turns, making it impossible for her to shift across the body. Frequently, the fairy is unable to reach the heart energy pot to fill it because the path is obscured by dark brown chocolate that the fairy can not see-through, and the dense candy traps the fairy's foot to the bottom. As a result, the individual who has consumed an excessive amount of candy and chocolate does not receive any energy in their heart pot.

When the fairy appears, she often discovers that the individual has been smoking cigarettes.

Oh, my God!

The fairy can't see something no matter where she goes. Clouds of dense smoke obscure the energy pots, and the individual only receive half of the energy because the fairy is lost in the smoke.

Fairies are tiny and fragile, yet with their magical abilities, they can defend themselves very well. They can't abide one thing, though.

The aroma of beer!

When someone enters and senses noisy snoring, they pick up their energy kettles and go to the next user. The individual who has been consuming beer has little stamina, and when they wake up in the morning, they have a bad headache, a nasty taste in their mouth, and their stomach feels like it is full of raw potatoes.

Fairies understand that when people snore, it is because they have been consuming alcohol, and they have a reasonable excuse not to offer these people more steam.

And when the fairy inserts their energy kettle into the person's mouth, the gases from the alcohol are very potent.

Do you know how fairies are extremely fragile creatures that depend on their magic to defend themselves?

Ok, sorcery does not operate against alcohol, and the fairies, being fragile, get as intoxicated as the individual who has drunk the beer when they breathe in the beer fumes. An intoxicated fairy with powerful supernatural abilities is a very bad fairy.

They always convert inebriated citizens into stone by mistake!

They can be seen everywhere; they are known as monuments in parks and museums.

As a result, people who consume junk food, drink a lot of alcohol, and smoke cigarettes are more likely to get sick.

Those that may not live a far happier existence.

So, the next time you consume too much candy, consider what the fairy who gets trapped in your mouth at night thinks about you!

The Origin of the Giraffe's Long Neck.

You might not believe it, but all giraffes had thin, short necks before Alonso was born. They didn't resemble giraffes at all because they had huge heads and short little bodies.

Alonso's parents brought him on a stroll around a large area known as a prairie when he was six months old. It was home to a variety of other species, including tigers, buffalo, and zebras.

Ha, ha, ha, ha, ha, ha, ha, ha, ha, ha, ha, ha, ha, ha, ha, ha, ha, ha, ha, ha His parents had a peek outside. Alonso was giggling his boots off despite the fact that nothing was amusing was happening.

Alonso's mother told his dad, "You'll have to carry him." I'm tired of taking up his sneakers.

Why are you kidding? Alonso's father couldn't find anything amusing.

I can't control myself, Alonso snorted. The grass tickles my tummy and lets me chuckle every time I take a step forward.

Alonso's father had small legs as well, but the grass did not tickle his tummy and make him scream, and he had never seen any giraffe that squealed with delight every time they went for a stroll.

Alonso's mother observed Alonso, who kept his head up high, as though he was afraid to let it slip near the ground.

It's because of the mushrooms. Alonso's father said. He despises the scent of them and tries to resist sniffing around them.

Alonso was also a nosy giraffe who loved to stick his neck over walls to see what was going on in the gardens of the other animals. In reality, between reaching away from mushrooms and peering over walls, Alonso had extended his neck by nearly a meter by the age of two.

It was all too good for Alonso to extend his neck like that, but something awful happened because of his huge head and weak little legs.

Assume Alonso is heading around a large open plain. And, suddenly, BIFF, BASH BOSCH!

A massive gust of wind smacks Alonso's long body, large ears, and tiny legs right in the center of his tummy. RUMBLE! BUMBLE! TUMBLE! RUMBLE! BUMBLE! RUMBLE! RUMBLE! RU Alonso, becoming so top-heavy, takes off.

That's grim, but things get much worse.

When he ages, his top becomes heavy, and his legs get thinner, and it just takes a sneeze in his path to bring Alonso tumbling over and over onto the next sector. And, when the wind was very high, his mummy and daddy had to bind Alonso to a tree to save him from blowing away!

The jungle doctor took one look at Alonso and recommended the best leg medication he had, and Alonso's little legs started to grow longer and longer within a few days.

Fantastic! Alonso sobbed. The lawn no longer tickles my stomach!

After a few weeks, they had grown so long that Alonso's father yelled STOP!

But the forest doctor was unable to intervene.

We'll avoid the drug, but it's so potent that his legs can keep rising for a little longer! Exclaimed the specialist.

So the leg treatment was discontinued, but Alonso proceeded to rise for the next two weeks, becoming taller and taller until he was the tallest giraffe in the household. He was so huge that he could see through the tops of trees!

Alonso awoke one morning, he spread his long legs and neck, stood up, and yawned, and then something odd occurred. Alonso stumbled away! Right on the tip of his nose!

The jungle doctor quickly recognized the issue.

You've been much more top-heavy with your long skinny legs, very large body, and broadhead.

As a result, the doctor administered some minor head medication to Alonso. This was done to shrink Alonso's head so he wouldn't tip over as he stood up.

The medication was successful, and Alonso's head started to shrink. When it was the scale that kept him from collapsing, the doctor offered him some stop the little head medication.'

As Alonso glanced in the mirror, he was taken aback. Two small horns had protruded from the top of his head, just behind his neck.

Which surprised me! The doctor was taken aback because there was no description of horns in the drug.

Alonso examined himself in the mirror once more. The tiny horns were very lovely.

The doctor said, "No problem!" Those will be gone too!

No way! Alonso examined himself in the mirror once more. They make me appear very dashing, and I intend to hold them.

Alonso was now the biggest and most elegant member of the tribe, and all the other female giraffes in the forest were smitten with him.

Yet, one of the female giraffes was smarter than the others. Arielle was her tag, and she realized that to pique Alonso's attention, she needed to make herself much more appealing than the other girl giraffes.

She realized she was very pretty in a small way and that if she decided to marry Alonso, she needed to be very pretty in a major way.

The jungle doctor was very considerate.

If Arielle grew to be the same height as Alonso, giraffes would be much larger and more graceful than the little podgy giraffes everybody was familiar with, so he decided to send Arielle the medication he had offered Alonso.

Oh my goodness! BANG! BANG! BANG! BANG! BANG! BANG! B WOWOOOOO!

A gorgeous, tall, slender, sleek, graceful, and trendy giraffe fluttered her eyelashes at Alonso six months back.

Arielle and Alonso were wed in the jungle church just weeks after Alonso's heart jumped.

Of course, their children were huge and beautiful, perhaps much taller than their parents. They had a fantastic existence. They had the most delicious leaves to eat from the tops of the plants. The happiest impression of all the creatures, and none of them had to do with the earthy smells that Alonso despised.

And, when each generation of Giraffes was bred, they grew taller and taller before we have the Giraffes we see today in Africa.

Alonso died several years ago, yet any time you see a giraffe with a long neck and tall legs, remember that it would not have occurred if it hadn't been for Alonso, who loved getting his tummy tickled by African grass, who was a very, very nosey giraffe, who hated the scent of mushrooms!

The Floating Baby

Oscar's parents were thrilled when he arrived. A smiling, bouncing, beaming infant who giggled and gurgled much of the time while he wasn't sleeping and looked like a tiny angel when he was asleep.

If you like to see what a little angel looks like because you are a nice little boy or girl, take a peek at yourself the next time you fall asleep, and you will be certain to see one!

On the other hand, Oscar did something that caused his mother to cry when he was two weeks old.

She yelled so loudly that the windows rattled, and that requires some effort!

Have you ever made your mother so angry that she screamed?

It's really simple; borrow an Elephant and drive it into the kitchen when she's preparing. It's an amusing thing to do that will get you laughing for weeks.

Oscar's mother cried as though he didn't have an elephant.

Jeffery, please! She screamed.

Oscar's father's name was Jeffery, which is presumably why she yelled it.

Take a look!

Julie, please! That was Oscar's mother's name; otherwise, Jeffery may have named someone else.

Jeffery was taken aback by Oscar's cot.

After all the crying, Oscar was already fast asleep, however, and this had surprised his parents; he was floating, six inches above his cot!

Babies aren't able to float! Jeffery took a deep breath.

Can you get how to gulp?

Assume you have a large amount of food in your mouth and take a huge swallow; if you're fortunate, you'll detect a kind of gurgle from your throat. That's a big gulp. When you do it, it gets louder and sends adults insane.

Oscar was still swimming, gulps or no gulps.

Julie screamed out, "Put a pair of books on his tummy!"

The books were successful. Oscar sank back into his cot, still quietly sleeping.

Babies don't float, said Jeffery once more.

Oscar's mother didn't respond because she couldn't take her gaze away from her boy, who was fast asleep under a couple of his storybooks.

As they removed the books from Oscar's tummy the next morning, he gently floated six inches above his cot.

They, of course, rushed him to the hospital. However, after an hour of checking on his monitor, the doctor declared that there was nothing in medical books about flying infants. But the doctor was a good guy, and even though he couldn't support him, he gave Oscar's parents some sound advice.

He said that you take him to the airport instead.

Oscar's parents felt it was a brilliant plan and hurried to the airport.

He's not a helicopter! At the airport, they smiled. "We know a lot about aircraft, but we don't know much about kids, including flying ones!

Oscar's parents brought him along, and you'll never guess what happened in the following weeks. Oscar drifted a little higher each day as he became bigger until his head was level with the windowsill!

If he is doing this, his nose will be hitting the roof after a few hours, his mother lamented.

And to feed him, we'll have to scale a rope! Grumbled his dad, who was still sore from trying to keep Oscar down as he bathed him.

And, one day, something happened that took them completely by surprise!

Oscar's mother will buckle him into his pushchair every morning before taking him for a stroll in the street. But on this specific morning, just when she was about to enter the park, she abruptly came to a halt. Her mouth opened wide, and she gaped. Can you get how to gape?

It is extremely easy. You stay perfectly still and let your mouth hang open, large and huge as it does when you eat breakfast, except without some food in it.

In the park, Oscar's mummy's mouth was gaping so big that she could hear the wind whistling through her teeth!

Oscar's pushchair seemed to float!

A floating pushchair is not permitted in the park! The parkkeeper was squeezing the pushchair with the large brush he used to dust up the leaves. You'll scare the ducks!

He reached into a bush and pulled out a large, hard stone, which he placed on top of the pushchair, causing it to sink to the bottom.

Oscar's mother reluctantly returned home, pushing her son and the large stone in front of her, asking when she might be able to take her son on a stroll now that she couldn't take him to the park with him anymore.

MrMc Donald's came from Scotland.

A Scotsman is a person born in Scotland. Scotland is a country in northern England where it gets so cold in the winter that people have to consume a lot of porridge to stay healthy to avoid getting swept away by the strong winds.

Mr. McDonald also stayed right next door to Oscar and his friends.

Why are you walking on a large piece of stone? Mr. McDonald stood by his gate while Oscar's mother passed by.

She clarified the situation in the park to the park keeper and the problem with Oscar, and how no one could help.

Mr. McDonald rubbed his sporran thoughtfully.

A sporran is a wispy piece of fabric that Scotsmen carry in front of their faces to itch while they dream.

When the wind was high, we used to have babies that flew about all over the house. Mr. McDonald said. Before we invented porridge, that is.

What is porridge? Oscar's mother was intrigued.

Porridge is made by stirring together oats and milk until the porridge is so dense that the spoon sticks up in the center of the dish.

Do you think giving Oscar some porridge will help him from floating? Oscar's mother was ecstatic; there was a slim possibility she would be able to save her son from swimming away.

Mr. McDonald was stroking his sporran once more. I know Scots that consume porridge, but it does not function on outsiders.

Oscar's mother and father searched high and low for any porridge that afternoon. But no one had learned about it anywhere they inquired, and in the evening, feeling very sad, they walked steadily home, porridge-less.

Mr. McDonald saw they were still driving the pram with the rock on top when he approached his gate.

Just don't answer me! He shook his head in disbelief, "The porridge doesn't fit!"

Oscar's parents shook their heads. "Anything can't succeed if you don't do it," Oscar's Mummy said.

We can't seem to locate some porridge! Oscar's father wept.

Mr. McDonald's eyes blinked. Why didn't you question me? He turned around and walked back to his building. I have a cupboard full of them!

Oscar's mother gently mixed a large bowl of porridge before the spoon stuck straight up in the center and watched as Oscar fed. He adored it, devouring every morsel in a matter of minutes.

When it came time to go to the park, his mother gently tied him into his pushchair and walked him there.

Still, she'd left everything out!

She remained motionless on the sidewalk, looking in awe at Oscar's pushchair. She'd forgotten about the stone!

Still, it didn't make a difference! The pushchair was not a floating item!

She brought Oscar out and gently opened her arms around him. "Oh my goodness!

Oscar just laid there like every other newborn – he wasn't floating!

The porridge had been successful!

Oscar's parents sent Mr. McDonald the world's largest container of lemonade as a sweet thank you.

Oscar also enjoys porridge every day, as does his father on very windy days. Oscar's mummy, on the other hand, never does because mummies are still controlling their weight.

The Dog, Cat, Hamster, and Parrot

Johnnie's mother and father adored animals. They adored them so much that their home was overrun with dogs. Full, full, full, full, full, full, full, full, full, full, full, full There was a pet in every room because the house was so full.

Carrot, a smiling, tail-wagging little puppy, was in the kitchen. He was nicknamed Carrot because he preferred carrots and because he was almost the same colour as one. Carrot chose to sleep in the kitchen since it was next to the back entrance. So he could keep an eye on it in case anyone who shouldn't be there came in. The carrot would then go crazy, rushing around the kitchen table, barking until his teeth clattered and everyone's ears ached!

The sailor was alone in the living room. If I told you Sailor had a long tail, big whiskers, purred when stroked, and drank tea, you'd believe me. I'm sure you can guess what kind of animal it was. It didn't have a trunk because it couldn't be an elephant, and it didn't have black and white markings, so it couldn't be a zebra because it wasn't big enough to be a giraffe.

As a result, Sailor may only be...

Yes, you guessed correctly!

The sailor was a feline.

Since it was the warmest and cosiest space in the building, Sailor stayed in the sat room.

Johnnie's pet was in little Jonnie's bed. It was short, tan, and fluffy, and it would spend hours running around in a wheel at the side of its cage for exercise.

I won't really go into it, so everybody understands what a hamster looks like. And Johnnie's hamster was called Harry because it sounded nicer than Horatio or Horace the hamster, and Cdefinitely better than Hobildygobildygibildygook, the hamster.

When the family was eating breakfast in the morning, there was always whooshing and flapping of wings.

Billy, the blackbird, was on his way! Since the blackbird was a wild bird, Johnnie's mother and father weren't sure whether it was named Billy, so they needed a name for it, and Billy and blackbird suit the bill nicely.

Billy used to strut about under the breakfast table, grabbing crumbs and bits, which made Jonnies mother really happy. It spared her the trouble of trying to clean up after tea!

But there was a unique pet in the space. It sat in a corner on top of a long thin pole with a perch on top. It had wings, several various colored feathers, and a broad hooked beak. It had yellow circles around its eyes and was effective at imitating what people said.

You're supposed to claim the pet was a parrot.

It was a parrot, according to the man who sold it to Johnny's dad.

Johnny's mother thinks it's a parrot.

Both the milkman and the postman claim it's a parrot.

They can't all be false, and you can't be either, so the pet in the hall must be a parrot.

The parrot's name was to be Fred, according to Johnnie's aunt. However, Fred, the parrot, does not sound very friendly. Johnnies mother tried to name it Polly, but everybody names their parrots Polly, and she was afraid that if she called out for Polly, hundreds of parrots would appear out of nowhere.

So they named the parrot Penelope; it may have been a boy parrot, but there was no way of knowing, so they went for a girl's name.

Penelope stayed in the hall where she could keep an eye on the front door and squawk loudly if someone who shouldn't be there walked in.

So the family had several dogs, which was going to cause Johnny's father a lot of surprises one day.

Johnnie's father had had a whizz boom day on this specific day! A whizz-bang day is the greatest kind of day to get when everything goes as planned. And because Johnnie's father was having such a whizz-bang day, he decided to call Johnny and his mother and invite them all out to a whizz-bang restaurant where Johnny might have whizz-bang chicken and chips and great ice cream.

What's up? He spoke into the phone.

What's up? A voice responded. It was a voice Johnny's father had never experienced before, and when it spoke on his phone, Johnny's father was taken aback.

Who is he? Enquired Johnnie's dad.

It's Carrot, said the voice in a strange barking accent.

The carrot was the name of the family's puppy, and dogs, of course, cannot communicate, but Johnnie's father was so shocked to hear Carrot speak that he, too, could not speak. He couldn't help but sputter.

Can you get how to sputter?

It would help if you first shut your mouth, but not too firmly. Now, breathe in through your nose, and then, and here comes the enjoyable part, blow all the air out through your teeth, causing your lips to flap.

It's much cooler if you sputter while you're eating. Little bits scatter about the place, making everybody chuckle – besides, of course, your mummy and daddy.

As a result, Johnny's father spluttered, then sprayed again.

What's up? The barky accent had improved this time. This new voice had a silky, creamy, and purring quality to it.

Who is he? Johnnie's father's spluttering had ceased, but his eyes were still wide with confusion.

The word is a sailor.

What about the cat?

Who else is there?

Johnny's father was staring at the screen. His dog and now his cat were both talking to him! His whizz bang day had suddenly transformed into a higgledy-piggledy what's going on here kind of day.

Is it okay if I talk with Johnny's mother? He reasoned that if he talked to Johnny's mum, he would demonstrate that he was not going insane when speaking to animals that were interacting but, as we all know, couldn't speak.

She went shopping.

What the heck! Johnny's father sprung into his seat. It was another speech, high and squeaky this time.

What is this person? He screamed.

The high-pitched voice was now pleased to be Harry. Don't you recognize a hamster when you see one?

But hamsters, cats, and dogs cannot communicate! Johnny's father was jumping up and down on his bottom, causing large dents in the seat of his chair. He'd even forgotten about taking Johnny and his mother out to eat.

I'm on my way home! He yelled.

We'll see you again! Harry said.

Johnny's father sped off, nearly tripping off the doormat when he rushed through the front gates.

Johnny's mother and Johnny were having their tea time slice of toast in the dining room when BANG! The door had slammed shut!

Johnny's father stood there, flushed and trembling.

Carrot sprang from the couch and raced to meet him, her tail wagging wildly. Johnny's father took her in his arms and kept her at arm's length.

So, what do you have to say now? He made a demand. Carrot looked at Johnny, then at Johnny's parent, perplexed as to why she was being dangled in the breeze.

Come on, let's go! Johnny's father pressed his nose against Carrot's. So, what do you have to say now?

Carrot didn't mention something, only licking Johnny's father's nose with her lips.

Sailor, the cat, entered the bed, perplexed as to what all the fuss was about.

You, too! Johnny's father placed Carrot down and listened to Sailor. "Have you already damaged your tongue?"

Johnny's mother was taken aback by her husband's reaction.

What in the world are you on about? She enquired.

Carrot, Sailor, and Harry have been calling! Daddy said.

What are you talking about? Mummy said.

What are you talking about? Johnny said.

The sailor gave a long sniff as though she was dreaming about it when Carrot just stared.

And they both burst out laughing! Except for Daddy.

Animals are unable to communicate! Mummy and Johnny sobbed.

However, they did! Daddy yelled.

Someone was talking on the phone in the kitchen, and there was a ringing noise.

There was the rattle of the phone being picked up before daddy could even switch.

What's up?

Daddy was taken aback by mummy's beauty. That's his voice responding! He hadn't even spoken a single phrase!

Thank you, just not yet. The voice went on.

Daddy turned around and walked down the hall on tiptoe.

Good-by. The phone rang and rang and rang and rang and rang and rang and

Johnny and Mummy grinned as they pushed into the hall with Daddy.

Daddy was stunned and stared in surprise.

It's Penelope calling! He exclaimed. Both of the voices are being imitated by the parrot!

Johnny and Mummy began to chuckle some more.

Good morning! Croaked Penelope, this time in the accent of her parrot.

Mummy smiled as she explained that she had just learned to talk. "And she will now pick up the phone with her claw."

You remember, Daddy said. Penelope is a very intelligent bird; she can do about all we do, but there is one thing she excels in that we cannot.

Mummy and Johnny exchanged glances with Daddy and then with Penelope.

What exactly is it? Mummy and Johnny were both asked.

By default, fly. Daddy laughed.

Penelope exclaimed, "You're right!"

Do you remember what happens then? Mummy was the first to chuckle, followed by Johnny, and finally by Daddy. Carrot turned over on her stomach and gave a doggy giggle; sailor hopped on the table and performed a pussycat dance, Harry did three somersaults in his cage, but Penelope remained perfectly still on her perch. When everybody had finished laughing and smiling, she immediately flapped her wings together in applause, overjoyed that she had arrived at such a funhouse.

Uncle Ben

Wendy assumed her Uncle Ben was completely insane. Since he was an engineer, her Uncle didn't have a typical career.

A designer creates inventions that have never been created before.

As in the room you're sleeping in. Someone got tired of sleeping standing up one day, but the ground was too stiff and rough to lie on. They had created a bed by taking a large piece of wood and placing four legs on each corner.

But it wasn't so good; the wood was as stiff as the earth and almost as rough, yet everyone else had the bright idea of placing something soft on the bed and sitting on it. It was much stronger, but lying in bed as the wind blowing was cold. So, one day, everyone else drew a sheep on top of themselves - just not a whole sheep! It is very wet and is called a sheep's skin since it is just outside the sheep. But the pine, the wings, the soft bit, and the sheepskin totally transformed the bed. Since it was so comfortable, everybody else imitated it, and now everybody has a room.

But inventing inventions is difficult; the bed took three inventors to develop. Wendy's Uncle, on the other hand, did not create beds; he was not that insane. What would be the purpose in inventing something that already existed?

Wendy's Uncle used to make weird and wonderful inventions. Like ice cream that didn't melt and didn't need to be held in the freezer. A TV with no echo so as not to annoy the neighbors. For the deaf, there was even an alarm clock that beat you over the head when it was time to get up.

But it wasn't Wendy's Uncle Ben's stupid inventions that made her realize he was as nuts as a fruitcake.

He used to converse with his equipment.

She would always accompany him to his studio. However, she still perched on a high stool, far out of her Uncle's path.

Hammer, come on! Let's see what you've got, hammer! Her Uncle will yell. Wendy would wait, mouth agape, as Uncle raised the hammer high and then slammed it down with a thud. It sailed past the nail he was attempting to hammer and created a large dent in the wood he was attempting to nail.

What a jerk! Look at what you've accomplished! He roared and shook the hammer in front of his face, glaring at it. You should do more than that!

The hammer will sail through the air once more, this time slamming the nail through the wood.

Wendy, you'll see that if you speak to your instruments, they'll function even more for you. And her uncle will gently and lovingly put his hammer back in his huge red tool case.

Now, tool case, you look after my ax, he'd suggest as he shut the door of the large red crate. Then he'd place the large red box on top of his workbench.

Here, job table, you're in charge of my huge red toolbox. He would carefully lock the door of his workshop with a large key from his pocket and hang the key on a hook, meaning, key, you sit there before I come back and use you again.

Wendy used to laugh as her Uncle spoke in that manner; it was as though he was speaking to a blank stone.

Wendy's Auntie didn't find it amusing when her husband referred to his tools; she simply assumed Wendy had married a clown who had abandoned his circus.

A spanner is a long piece of metal with a shaped end that fits over a bolt. Bolts are small, circular pieces of metal that tie objects together, but they can only be undone with a large piece of metal known as a spanner.

Uncle had a massive array of spanners, all vibrant and shiny, hung across the walls of his workshop, each one a different size with all the different types of bolts.

Auntie had screamed of a rattling noise while driving, and Uncle discovered a bolt had fallen loose under her window.

Come on, spanner, we've got stuff to do! He bent under the sea, fitted the spanner onto the bolt, and pushed after retrieving the right size spanner.

And do you remember what happened?

There is nothing.

The bolt did not budge no matter how much Uncle tugged.

What's the deal for you? The spanner was screamed at by Uncle. "Let's get to work, let's get to work!"

Wendy observed as Uncle became more irritated until, with much effort, Uncle let out an extra heave.

And do you remember what happened?

A loud crack rang out.

The spanner had been shattered in two!

Uncle raged on the spot until he couldn't take it any longer and hurled the shattered spanner again.

Do you remember what happens then?

The spanner sailed through the garden and kicked his garden gnome's head off!

Screwdrivers! You're useless! Uncle yanked all the gleaming spanners from the wall with a wave of his arms and tossed them into the trash. And, his face flushed with fury, he went to the hardware store and purchased a whole new shiny box full of new spanners. He took the one for the bolt on the car seat and began to tug and pull after carefully arranging them on the wall. Nothing occurred this time; the bolt failed to turn.

DOODLE DOO! YANGLETANGLE DOODLE DOO! He screamed. That is a one-of-a-kind word.

And it is only used by Uncles when they are furious and brimming with anger. It's a phrase they yell as they're about to pop.

Auntie dashed out the door.

Do you remember what happens then?

Uncle threw the new spanner backward, knocking the head off his other garden gnome!

Uncle was still spinning about in circles, tossing his arms in the air like a broken windmill.

What exactly is the problem? Auntie sobbed.

Uncle yelled, "These latest spanners don't fit, even though I talk to them!"

Auntie examined the spanner that had struck the garden gnome. She then began to chuckle. This irritated Uncle even more, and he began to jump like a human Kangaroo.

What's the big deal? He yelled.

Can you communicate in Chinese? Auntie inquired.

Uncle spat, "Of course not."

Auntie chuckled, "Maybe you'd best learn." These spanners were manufactured in China, and I had little idea what you're saying.

Auntie was about to chuckle again when she realized what she had just written. Perhaps she was as enraged as Uncle!

Mr. Vegetable

All addressed Mr. Vegetable as Mr. Vegetable. And the fact that it was not his real name. Before he and his family moved into the house on the corner, it had a lovely garden in the center, down the road, and in the back.

But, Oh No! Mr. Grey, Mr. Vegetable's real name, disliked roses, beautiful bushes, and lovely plants. They were all gone within a month, and in their place was... do you guess? Instead of flowers, bushes, and leaves, what did Mr. Grey plant?

Vegetables, too!

Rows of onions, lettuces, and potatoes were planted in the front yard. Bright red tomatoes and runner beans climbed the side and up the building, while big green cabbages, turnips, and just about everything else grew in the back.

As a result, all of Mr. Grey's neighbors wanted to refer to him as Mr. Vegetable!

Lucinda, Mr. Vegetable's 5-year-old baby, was a lovely young lady with a serious issue. She was a sad little kid.

She was dissatisfied because of her father. Mr. Vegetable was a strict guy who disliked flowers and little girls who desired everything they saw, including Lucinda.

May I get some ice cream, Daddy?

No, Lucinda, you've only had two this week!

May I have a new pencil, Daddy?

No, Lucinda, the one you have is always fine.

As a result, anytime Lucinda asked for something, her father still replied no. Lucinda's sadness grew over the weeks, and she used to go up to her bedroom several days and weep for a long time. But Mr. Vegetable was not sad; in fact, he looked much worse and was on the verge of tears himself because he was so concerned.

His beautiful green cabbages had abruptly shifted, the rich green had vanished, and the cabbages were turning all white and shrinking. The red tomatoes had reached the peak of the wall and were beginning to slip down to the earth. The potatoes had stopped rising, and the runner beans had abruptly stopped working.

Mr. Vegetable was so concerned about missing his prized vegetables that he summoned the gardener from the nearby park.

The park garden was a specialist in everything, including vegetable cultivation. He started with the lettuce and onions, then moved on to the sad old tomatoes, and finally scratching his head over the cabbages.

Bending back, he took a pinch of dirt and crumbled it between his fingertips, sniffed it, and shook it. He moved slowly around the building, stopped, and then walked around it again.

He finally stared up at the stars, removed his glasses, wiped them with his handkerchief, then looked up again.

That is your problem, sir. His index finger was straight up in the clouds. That is unquestionably your problem.

Mr. Vegetable raised his head. He couldn't see the sky because of a storm above, so even though he did, he couldn't fathom how it could be creating trouble with his crops.

But when he looked down, the gardener had vanished.

If you're having problems with the moon, the police sergeant advised. You never annoy us here at the police station. We don't do skyscrapers.

So, who do I see? Mr. Vegetable wept; he had been looking for someone to support him with his sky for a week and had tried the police since he had run out of ideas.

The only people I know who know something about the sky are weathermen, said the sergeant. He then closed his counter with a flourish and headed to the police station canteen for a cup of tea.

They stared at Mr. Vegetable oddly at the weather station.

The weatherman said that no one has a problem with the sky. But after hearing about Mr. Vegetable's vegetables and what the park's gardener had claimed, he decided and came to Mr. Vegetable's house to see what was wrong.

He started with the vegetables in the front yard, then moved on to the sinking tomatoes on the field, and finally to the sickly cabbages.

First, he rubbed his nose and smiled up at the moon.

That's odd, he exclaimed.

38

What's odd about this? Mr. Vegetable even glanced up at the stars, but he stayed next to the weatherman in case he disappeared like the park gardener.

It is a cloud.

Mr. Vegetable could see the storm, but it seemed to him no more from any other cloud.

Your building is the only one on the street with a cloud over it. The weatherman was pacing in a circle on the sidewalk, looking up. Because of the fog, the crops are starving because they do not have enough sun.

The weatherman stepped into the sun next door to get heated to figure out what was going on since the day was meant to be light and clear, not dull and gloomy as it was in Mr. Vegetable's backyard.

Mr. Vegetable stood on a garden bench, watching the weatherman pace up and down the street. He stepped through the sunlight, then under the fog, back into the sunlight, and then back into the cloud. He repeated this three times before abruptly stopping.

Mr. Vegetable could see the weatherman's grin stretched over his face from where he was.

The element of water! The weatherman yelled. "That's why you have a cloud." You have an excessive amount of water in your building."

Of course, Mr. Vegetable knew that water was needed to create a cloud, but there was one issue. He didn't get much more rainfall than anyone else because there were no clouds over their windows.

And something is leaving the air damp, according to the weatherman.

May I have a cat, Daddy? Every one of my friends has a cat.

Mr. Vegetable was enraged because Lucinda had emerged from the house and disturbed the weatherman.

No, you can't, because I'm extremely distracted.

Lucinda sobbed uncontrollably. She sobbed into the building as she screeched her way along the garden road.

The weatherman was taken aback. Should she weep like that all the time? He inquired.

She is always moving and never sleeps. Mr. Vegetable snapped his fingers.

Why is it that she is unable to have a pet? Mr. Vegetable seemed stern to the weatherman.

Because...because...because...because...because...because...because...because...because...because Mr. Vegetable thought furiously, but no matter how much he thought, he couldn't think of an excuse for his daughter not to have a cat.

Why don't you give her a cat and any of the other stuff she likes, said the weatherman, and I hope you'll see your vegetables growing again."

Mr. Vegetable stared at the weatherman as if he were mad. How is it possible? He let out a snort.

You give it a shot, and I'll check in with you in a week to see how your vegetables are doing. The weatherman said as he closed the garden gate behind him.

For the next week, if Lucinda needed something, Mr. Vegetable considered it very deeply, and since she was a good little kid, she wasn't too selfish and didn't ask for too much, so her father didn't have to consider too hard very much before saying yes.

When the weatherman returned a week later, the first thing he noticed was a tiny ball of fluff racing down the street to reach him.

Lucinda smiled, "It's fluffy, my latest kitten." The weatherman believed Lucinda had improved. She seemed to be even more animated and cheerful now. And I've had ice cream every single day this week! She laughed. It's so sweet that Daddy has avoided telling no.

They're growing back! Mr. Vegetable extended a soft handshake to the weatherman. Could you take a peek at my beautiful veggies?

The cabbages were now green, and the tomatoes were lovely and red and creeping up the wall; in reality, all of the vegetables seemed to be in good health.

How did it happen? Mr. Vegetable inquired.

The weatherman raised his finger in the same manner as the park ranger.

Mr. Vegetable exclaimed, "It's off!" The cloud has vanished.

And it had, the sky was blue with big yellow sun in the center warming and growing all the plants in Mr. Vegetable's yard.

Since Lucinda is no longer crying! The weatherman laughed. When she cried so hard, everything became so wet that it produced the cloud you had over your home.

Mr. Vegetable could only think of one thing to tell thank you to the weatherman.

Will you figure out what he got him?

Remember, he has a beautiful vegetable garden.

I'll inform you if you haven't guessed. It was a bottle of the forecaster's favorite whiskey.

HAHAHAHAHAHAHAHAHAHAHAHAHAHAHAHAHA

Didn't you think I was going to suggest he brought him a bowl of vegetables?

Pricilla

Pricilla was a neat and precise little kid. Her mother and father were concerned that she was too detailed and neat. As she was at the table, she would make sure the knives and forks were completely straight and would fiddle with them until they were. When her dinner came, she would place her meat on the right side of her plate, her potatoes on the left, and her greens in a tidy little square in the middle.

Have you ever seen her bedroom? If you haven't, let me remind you about it.

Many of her dolls, including her toy telephone and magic hairbrush, are still stored in a large box in the corner until she has finished playing with them. Her clothes are all on hangers in her closet, and the hangers are all hung in a line, giving the impression that her clothes are queuing to get out.

The huge red rug on the floor stopped exactly by her room because when she takes her slippers off before going to bed, her feet do not hit the cold floor, and she also begged her daddy to make a little box to place her slippers in, so she could slip them under the bed because they looked untidy when she took them off! That's a lot of neatness!

She couldn't sleep in a bed until the sheet was precisely under her little chin and the bedsheets were close and soft.

When her mother walked in to kiss her goodnight, the kiss had to be in the center of her forehead. Otherwise, Pricilla would mumble for half an hour before falling asleep.

I know what you're saying. Little girls have many dolls to play with, and I haven't even included Pricilla's dolls.

You're not going to accept what I'm about to tell you. I, too, didn't believe that before I saw it. In reality, I had to pinch my leg to make myself move just to make sure I wasn't hallucinating. Can you ever squeeze your knee to force yourself to jump? It's great for making sure you're not sleeping or dreaming. But pinching your leg hurts, so it's easier to pinch someone else's to watch them jump.

Pricilla's bedroom had a long shelf. And when I say "broad," I mean it. If you spread your arms out to look how far apart your hands are, it is very long, yet Pricilla's shelf was much larger. Longer than your mother spreads out her harms and much longer than your father stretches out his arms!

And the shelf was brimming with... you'll have to guess then. What are the favorite toys of a little girl? What do they most often interact with? You'll know right away if I inform you the name of their favorite toy starts with D.

Well, indeed!

Dolls, please!

And Priscilla had a number of them, all lined up on this tall, long shelf.

But it wasn't the most impressive part. You'll have to think about it and try and picture it now.

Imagine all the dolls lying in a straight line, their tiny legs hanging off the shelf's edge!

Consider the dolls joining hands with one another!

They were holding each other's hands and turning their heads into Pricilla's room as though they were watching her sleep!

But it wasn't why they were all staring at Pricilla. She had strategically set them so that each night before she went to bed, she could look at each of her dolls and say good night to them individually!

That's an excellent thing to do. I'm sure you don't say goodnight to each of your toys before going to bed. In reality, most children nowadays have so many toys that they can stay up all night saying goodnight to them!

But that is not the point of this novel.

Priscilla awoke one day sneezing, then she sneezed every few minutes, and we all know what that says, don't we?

Pricilla had contracted a cough, so she went to the hospital.

Pricilla was also occupied in the doctor's waiting area. Arranging all magazines into orderly little piles, tidying up the games for the kids to play with, and even inspecting the curtains to ensure they stayed straight in the windows.

She's an immaculate little child; her mother told the doctor as he inspected Pricilla. She must keep it in order.

He examined her throat first, then felt her jaw, and eventually took her temperature.

Pricilla was sitting at the doctor's desk, filled with documents, journals, and other things used by physicians.

Priscilla abruptly rose to her feet. She remarked, "The workspace is untidy." Can I clean it up?

The doctor burst out laughing. Thank you so much, Pricilla! He smiled. But you better lend me your thumb because I'd like to test your blood.

Doctors measure people's blood to see what kind of cold they have and how to treat it. Taking Pricilla's thumb, he pricked it so lightly that she didn't note, then rubbed her thumb against a piece of plastic, which he then protected with another piece of plastic, and do you realize what was between the elements of plastic?

A glob of Priscilla's semen, a red blob!

Now I will get you better; the doctor grinned as he gently placed the piece of plastic in his drawer. "If you come back tomorrow, I'll offer you some medication, and you'll be able to quit sneezing in no time.

Pricilla's mother stood up and walked to the entrance, but Pricilla remained motionless.

Come on, her mother said, the doctor has another patient.

Pricilla remained motionless.

What the hell is going on? Asked the doctor, while Pricilla, who was concerned, remained motionless.

Pricilla rose softly, took her mother's hand in hers, and whispered in her ear. Her mother glanced at Priscilla, and at the psychiatrist, before breaking up laughing.

You remember how I said Pricilla is neat and likes to hold anything in its place?

The doctor gave a smile.

Ok, doctor, she's so concerned about leaving everything behind that she'd like to ask you a question.

Pricilla returned and stood by the doctor's desk, and the doctor grinned.

Could you please give me my blood back, doctor? She muttered something.

Both the doctor and Pricilla's mother burst out laughing.

Pricilla was now ultra duper tidy.

MrNotsure

MrNotsure was a bit of a stumbling block. In reality, he was more than a tad bit of a problem; he was a major tad bit of a problem, and he was gradually making his family insane. His dilemma was, and there lay the rub, no one understood what it was! It was just that it was a concern.

When he went out, he would lock the front door, then pause halfway down the garden route, thought hard, and then turn around and confirm if he had closed the door.

At the front gate, he'd turn around and run back up the road, rattle the fence, and stroll back down the street, relieved that it was still closed. Halfway down the lane, he'd come to a halt, thought long, then, you know it, sprint back to his front door.

This was very exhausting for all, including MrNotsure.

When he was in bed at night, he would whine about being tired before turning off the lamp. And he'd switch on the light again to double-check that he'd switched it off!

His coffee was often so hot that no one could drink it at breakfast. This was due to MrNotsure's habit of putting the coffee three times to ensure he hadn't neglected to bring it in the first time.

He was said to take four showers, one after the other, not to ensure cleanliness, but to ensure he hadn't missed the first!

He would always stand at the bus stop and watch three buses pass past without boarding either of them because he wasn't sure which one was the best one for him.

His mom, MrsNotsure, erupted one day because he was doing it twice, even three times.

Have you ever seen anyone blow up? Explode so violently that they cling to the ceiling? Fortunately, it doesn't happen too much, although it did on this particular day.

VISIT A DOCTOR IMMEDIATELY! MrsNotsure yelled. ADD TO THAT, Without DOING It TWICE!

MrNotsure climbed a ladder and gently lowered MrsNotsure from the ceiling, patting her back to settle her down. He then patted her head again to ensure that it was well patted.

GET OFF! MrsNotsure roared and erupted once more, this time to the ceiling.

The doctor observed MrNotsure enter his surgery, sit down, stand up, leave, return, and sit down again.

I'm doing it twice, MrNotsure said, crossing his ankles, uncrossing them, and then crossing them again.

Doubledetwicefluenza is an abbreviation for doubledetwicelyfluenza. The psychiatrist mumbled.

Please excuse me. MrNotsure double-checked the doctor's lips to ensure he hadn't spoken such a long term.

Doubledetwicedetwicedetwicedetwicedetwicedetwicedet, The doctor repeated it. "That's the medical term for repeating anything."

MrNotsure was given a prescription for certain pills that would solve his dilemma. The doctor said that the tablets are extremely potent. You may not exceed two a day.

MrNotsure traveled to two pharmacies to buy his pills, which was entirely natural given that he had not yet begun taking his medication.

Two days later, the doctor received a phone call from a lady who was yelling at him. MrsNotsure was the name of the lady.

I'm going insane! She exclaimed.

Oh my goodness! The doctor held the phone away from his ear; MrsNotsure was screaming so violently that it caused his cheeks to tremble!

"It's because of the pills you sent my husband!" "Have they taught him to do anything twice? The doctor was questioned.

Oh, they've made him forget to do something twice, MrsNotsure frothed.

He's not doing it now! MrsNotsure screamed. He has forgotten how to get out of bed!

How many tablets has he taken? The psychiatrist felt he understood what went wrong.

"First he takes two, as you instructed him, then he takes another two in case he forgets the first two!" MrsNotsure clarified.

As a result, if he needs half as many drugs, he can forget twice as many. The doctor now understood just what was to be accomplished.

You must inform him that he should only take one pill at a time. And he'll take another in case he forgets about the first, bringing the total to two, the correct amount of tablets!

MrsNotsure called the doctor again two days later, although this time she was not shouting; instead, she was laughing, but the doctor couldn't see that while she was on the phone.

It's fantastic, doctor; MrNotsure is just doing it once now, which is a huge relief.

The doctor was thrilled that he had helped another customer, so much so that he allowed himself chocolate from the box he kept on his desk for when he was feeling good about himself. In reality, he took two chocolates this time. In case he didn't eat the first one!

Mrs. Green's Friend

Mrs. Green was nicknamed Mrs. Green not because she was green but because she was Mrs. Green.

You couldn't possibly get green folk, can you? If people were orange, you'd presume they were peas and throw them in a pot to roast. You can't just run about frying people.

But it's a good thing Mrs. Green was just named Mrs. Green because that's what her mother and father's names were.

If you meet someone who goes by the name Mr. Yellow? I don't, which is a good thing; otherwise, they might be mistaken for bananas, and people will peel them!

I know a Mr. Pink, a Mr. Black, and even a Mr. Grey. But I've never seen someone named Mr. Red, Mrs. Blue, or Mr. Purple. That doesn't matter because we were worried about Mrs. Green.

Mrs. Green desired a rabbit. She desired a companion who could pet and pat, take on walks, and chat while alone.

Still, and this was the issue, she had no idea what kind of dog she needed. Did she want a large dog who barked at visitors and guarded her house? Did she like a little dog she might take around, one who barked at people and then concealed behind her blouse? Or did she like a medium-sized dog that barked at the intruder and then bolted up to her skirt?

Mrs. Green, on her way to the pet store, had to cross the park. However, she did not.

Get the message through. Suddenly, halfway through, she came to a halt and gazed, her eyes wide open in confusion, and the man is standing next to her, prepared to grab them if they popped out.

There was a note at the path's end. 'NO DOGS ARE ALLOWED!' Where was she supposed to take the dog for a stroll if she purchased one? When she passed the store, another sign on the door said, 'NO DOGS ALLOWED!' Also, there was a sign at the subway station that said, 'NO DOGS ALLOWED!'

This was serious; nobody wanted dogs anywhere, so Mrs. Green opted not to purchase a dog instead of having another cat.

I'll bet you an ice-lolly stick you'll never guess what Mrs. Green got for a cat!

Does it help if I inform you she saw her potential pet in the park?

Does it benefit that she sees it floating in a pond in the park?

Even the big toe would realize what she had bought if she found it floating in a pond in the park and heard squawking.

Well, indeed! What a duck!!

You know, if there were ducks in the park, she could take the duck for a stroll there, and if there was no 'NO DUCKS ALLOWED' sign on the store or the subway, she could take the duck shopping. As well as for a trip on the train!

She brought her duck around, carefully picking a sweet collar and leash, and spent a peaceful evening stroking and chatting to her duck, and as a special treat, she packed her bath with water and let the duck sleep in it!

She brought her duck for a stroll in the park the next morning, bright and early. The Park Keeper appeared surprised when Mrs. Green lead her duck down to the pond's side but said nothing because his park did not have a 'NO DUCKS ALLOWED' sign.

Then something awful happened.

No way! Mrs. Green did not slip and fall in the pond! That would not be terrible; however, it would be amusing.

The duck wriggled its jaw, shook its head, and slipped free from the collar!

Mrs. Green was taken aback by the empty collar. Still, and this is the sad part, her duck had disappeared when she looked up.

It'd swum down to all of the other ducks in the pond! Mrs. Green couldn't tell which duck belonged to her since ducks all look the same.

The Park Keeper couldn't support because he was paying to look after gardens, not ducks, so Mrs. Green walked steadily home, her bare collar and lead trailing behind her.

Now we have to wonder what Mrs. Green's next pet was!

Would it help if I inform you the pet had around, little head?

You should know right away if I inform you it had wings, could fly, was grey, and cooed.

Well, indeed! Mrs. Green purchased a pigeon!

She attached a very fine yarn to one of its legs and let it sit on her window sill all day, shuffling up and down and cooing because it was so content.

Mrs. Green, on the other hand, was dissatisfied that she had a cat she couldn't take on walks and one that drove her insane with its cooing.

Mrs. Green screamed at the pigeon to avoid cooing at the top of its lungs one day, then the neighbor shouted at Mrs. Green for shouting, and his neighbor shouted at him for shouting.

Mrs. Green, enraged at all the confusion her pigeon was making, went into the kitchen, picked up a large knife, dashed back to the pigeon, and lifted the knife over her head.

You'll never guess what Mrs. Green did now.

She murdered the pigeon!

No, she didn't. Mrs. Green is far too sweet to murder something! She lowered the knife and swoosh! Remove the string from the pigeon's tail!

As it flew down, the pigeon was much happier because it could now coo anywhere and bother others!

Mrs. Green sat down and considered for a long time. What kind of pet will she carry on park hikes, into stores, and on trains?

Can you think she'll be able to afford an elephant? She could, but they were so large that she couldn't push them through her front door.

She might purchase a tiger, but it would devour anyone, even Mrs. Green.

She might get a rat, but you can't take a mouse, hamster, or squirrel on a stroll.

It's a squirrel!

As a bird, I'd like to get a squirrel.

That would be particularly absurd since squirrels live in trees and eat nuts, and Mrs. Green lacked both trees and nuts.

Mrs. Green stared at the animals in the pet store, and they all looked so sweet and cheerful that she decided to purchase them all. The puppies, especially one little fuzzy puppy, came racing across the room and leaped into her arms.

The manager of the pet shop introduced him as Henry. "He's the sweetest pet in the entire place."

Mrs. Green pulled out her credit card and purchased the puppy before she realized what she was doing!

She couldn't bear leaving the little package behind.

The NO DOGS ALLOWED signals, though, remained. Mrs. Green was unable to drive her little dog anywhere.

Mrs. Green then noticed an illustration in a travel journal one day. She stared at the photo three times, each time laughing a little more; before the third time, she let out a whoop and clapped her hands in the air!

She could now carry her dog to the park, the stores, and even on trains!

She then went to the craft store and purchased a package of modeling clay next to the DIY store and purchased a pot of paint of the same color as her dog and a piece of twine.

I'm sure you couldn't guess what Mrs. Green was going to do, could you?

She began by making two small mounds of modeling clay that she decorated with dog-colored paint, and then she added the small mounds to the dog. She put one behind its neck and the other in front of its little tail before taking the dog for a stroll in the forest.

The Park Keeper was enraged.

He yelled, "You can't carry dogs in here!"

Mrs. Green said, "I don't have a puppy."

What exactly is it? The Park Keeper yelled.

It's my little camel!

We all know that camels have two humps on their backs, much like the camel in Mrs. Green's image. And the Park Keeper realized dogs don't have two humps on their backs, but even if it seemed like a dog to him, he had to step aside to let Mrs. Green past because there was no sign that CAMELS NOT In.

And though the managers shook their heads as they noticed the two humps, it was the same in the store and on the train.

Mrs. Green was so impressed by how her proposal turned out that she is strongly considering adopting another puppy. But then she'll have to create two more humps!

The Woman in the Golden Shoes

Mr. Holloway was a wealthy individual. But, every year at the same period, he'd start to worry; he'd lay up at night, unable to sleep because he couldn't stop dreaming.

At work, where he was popular because he was the main boss, staff would often have to repeat the same stuff to him three or four times because he was just not listening; he would forget items like not drinking his tea, not fixing his shoelaces, and sometimes forgetting where he had left his vehicle!

All who met him could foresee what was about to occur. As Mr. Holloway gazed into space for hours, sat at his desk with his head between his knees, and sometimes stumbled into walls, there could only be one reason.

His wife was about to celebrate her birthday, and the trouble for Mr. Holloway was that he had no idea what to get her as a gift.

When you are very wealthy, you have anything you need because you should not need something more once you have everything you need.

Mrs. Holloway had all the clothing she could carry, and since she was a lady, she wasn't involved in sports so that she wouldn't want a football, or a race car, or a video game; she had an iPhone and a huge box of chocolates that she never ate, you can see Mr. Holloway's dilemma, Mrs. Holloway had all she could want, twice over.

Mr. and Mrs. Holloway were heading to the theatre that evening, and Mrs. Holloway immediately frowned as she was getting ready, all posh, so you have to be dressed smartly to go to the theatre.

You know, both of my shoes look the same, and I'd love to get a pair that didn't look like shoes.

Mr. Holloway did not pay much attention at first because, despite having over two hundred skirts, Mrs. Holloway complained that she never had something to wear when she prepared for a night out, which was a little silly, wasn't it? Mr. Holloway squeezed his eyes impatiently as she over fifty pairs of sneakers, which was a little ridiculous because he couldn't see what he was doing because he was tying his belt.

And... WHISH! BANG! WHACK! It struck him like a ton of bricks!

A genius concept – the solution to his dilemma!

Well, indeed!

His wife needed a pair of shoes that didn't look like shoes – he'd get her a pair for her birthday!

But the next day, he realized he had another minor issue. They would not be considered shoes if he purchased her a pair of shoes that did not look like shoes. But, how did he go about purchasing a pair of sneakers that weren't called shoes?

He might get her a bus or a doughnut! They haven't named shoes; they were called buses and doughnuts, but she couldn't put a bus or a doughnut on her foot because it would be crazy.

But, and this is why he was so wealthy, Mr. Holloway was a brilliant guy. What if he purchased her a pair of shoes made of material that shoes were not normally made? That would set them apart from any other shoes.

And it didn't take him long to figure out what it was.

It's gold!

He'd purchase a pair of gold shoes for his mom!

So how do you go about finding a pair of gold shoes when no one has any?

You've always created a pair.

Gold is so valuable that it is mostly used for very costly jewelry, and only the very, very wealthy can afford to purchase it. Mr. Holloway, on the other hand, was very wealthy.

The jeweler and valuable item maker couldn't support himself.

I make brooches, rings, and necklaces, he said, but I can't make shoes.

And the shoemaker replied, "I can only make shoes out of leather; no one has ever produced a pair of gold shoes."

Mr. Holloway was starting to pace in circles of worry again, the day of his wife's birthday approaching, and he still hadn't bought her a gift.

Without a doubt! He sobbed. "I'm ridiculous!" I don't need a jeweler or a shoemaker; this gift is so unique that it requires someone equally unique to create it!"

Do you meet someone so unique that he can create a pair of golden shoes? I'm sure you can't. However, I can.

A sculptor is anyone who makes sculptures.

A sculptor is a rather astute person. They will look inside a block of stone and see a statue. And they take a hammer and chip away at the rock, allowing everybody to see the statue!

It didn't take long for the sculptor to discover a block of gold containing a pair of shoes, and he was much faster to hammer the gold away so that he could give the gleaming gift to Mr. Holloway.

Mr. Holloway was ecstatic.

He had a beautiful wooden box lined with purple velvet designed to house the shoes, making them appear twice as beautiful. They were so magnificent, in reality, that they stole his breath away, forcing him to puff to keep up with his breathing.

As the day of his wife's birthday party approached, all of the guests were strolling around the house and yard, drinking champagne, as an ensemble performed on the terrace of Mr. Holloway's massive house and waiters moved among the guests with trays of delicious food.

Then Mr. Holloway emerged on the terrace and rang a small bell to draw the attention of his guests.

It's almost time to send my wife her birthday gift! He made an announcement. A waiter arrived, carrying the exquisite wood box on a tray as big as his face of much pomp and circumstance. Placing the tray in front of Mr. Holloway, he stood back as Mr. Holloway took the package and gave it to his wife with great pomp.

Her jaw fell open when she opened the package, and she looked in shock at her gift. The gift did more than just steal her heart away. It halted her breathing! She stumbled over, straight into a tub of jelly, with a flutter of her lashes!

When her girlfriend, who was standing behind her, saw the golden heels, she turned around and dropped backward in another feint of joy, this time into a trifle!

Mrs. Holloway couldn't afford to put on her golden heels, so the waiters immediately washed the jelly and trifled off her two sisters.

They were the most stylish pair of shoes she owned, and they completely matched her feet. Mt Holloway was so pleased that his wife adored the shoes that he requested that the ensemble perform his wife's favorite song. He walked out onto the terrace, turned in the middle, raised his arms, and asked his wife to dance.

She stood up, and stood up, and stood up, and stood up, and stood up, and stood up, and stood up, and stood up, and stood up, and stood up, and stood up Mr. Holloway fixed his gaze on his wife, who was swaying towards him but not going further.

I can't breathe, she exclaimed. Her feet seemed like they were nailed to the cement.

Oh my god, Mr. Holloway exclaimed.

With a thump, his wife fell back down in the jeans. They're trapped, and I can't run.

Gold is very strong, and the shoes were pure gold and much too heavy for Mrs. Holloway's little feet to travel.

Mr. Holloway did not pause. He directed the servants to remove the golden shoes.

"You will get your present back next week, my love," he exclaimed, "and I guarantee you will be willing to walk in your golden heels."

So the next week, Mr. Holloway threw another huge bash, and all the visitors, including his mom, couldn't wait to see what he'd made with the golden shoes.

The package was opened and delivered to Mrs. Holloway at the appropriate time. She didn't flinch when she opened the lid; instead, her face broke out in a big grin of delight.

She immediately pulled on the golden shoes she had taken out. Standing up, she glided to where her husband was waiting on the dance floor with a graceful gesture of her hand.

Everyone applauded and applauded Mr. Holloway.

Mr. Holloway had changed the golden shoes, making them much more special. He got them equipped with golden tires, and now his wife possessed the world's only pair of golden roller skates!

Grumpy King

The King was a very elderly King, with an almost old crown and a similarly aged Queen. He couldn't do much by himself because he was too old, so he needed many servants.

The King had been a very grumpy old King due to seeing so many subordinates who were constantly doing stuff incorrectly.

You ought to put a couple of them in the dungeons, said the Queen, who was much angrier than the King.

As a result, that evening, when one of the servants was serving soup to the monarch, the servant let out a big sneeze!

ATISHOOOOOO!

In anger, the soup splattered all over the King, who closed his eyes even harder than his bottom.

GET HIM IN THE DUNGEON! The King screamed.

No way! No, please, your Majesty! The servant begged, "Not the cellar!" All understood the castle's dungeon was a horrible location.

The dungeon was gloomy and damp, with water streaming down the walls, and the only food the inmates got to consume was the mushrooms that came out of the walls. It was the last spot everyone hoped to end up, with rodents racing across the floor and the clanking of the prisoner's chains.

The King yelled into the dungeon. Two guards pulled the weeping servant from the banqueting area, down the filthy staircase at the castle's base, and into the dungeon's black pit.

For the first time since Christmas, the Queen grinned. The King snorted, got up, and marched to his bed-chamber to change his soup-soaked uniform.

The King's dresser in the bed-chamber was taking a quiet drink of the King's bedtime sherry, knowing the King was already eating his supper.

"WHAT DO YOU THINK YOU'RE DOING?" The King walked in right as his dresser took a huge gulp from the sherry bottle.

The King was already screaming before he could react.

GO TO THE DUNGEON WITH THE THIEF!

Two more guards dashed up and dragged the screaming dresser down the steps, then down the dusty stairs at the bottom of the tower, before tossing the dresser into the dungeon's black pit.

The King wanted to go on a walk in his garden the following day. He was very proud of his garden, filled with lovely flowers and plants, but the King's favorite feature was his grass. It ran from the back of the castle down to the water, which belonged to the King as well.

He looked up down the great yard, which was as lush as grass could be, with no weeds or blemishes. Then, oh my goodness!

A mound of dead leaves, whirled around by a gentle wind, fell tumbling towards him. When he saw brown leaves on his green grass, the King's face turned crimson with anger, and he screamed and raced around in a circle, waving his arms.

The gardener, who had inadvertently flipped his wheelbarrow, scattering the leaves across the grass, blanched in fear.

TAKE HIM TO THE DUNGEON, roared the King, and watched as his garden was hauled across the yard, into the tower, down the dirty stairs at the bottom of the castle, and thrown into the dungeon's black pit.

Everyone in the castle and the surrounding village understood that the King would have them dragged down the dirty steps and thrown into the dungeon's black pit if they made an error. As a result, a tremendous peace descended on the castle. Servants crawled about on tiptoe if the King heard them and returned them to the cellar; cleaners swept the castle by hand in case the noise from the Hoovers irritated the king. Even the royal dustmen, the noisiest dustmen in the country, kept the dustbins far away from the castle before banging them dry.

On Monday, the King sent a chambermaid, a junior chef, and the postman (due to his delay) to the dungeon.

He sent his plumber, a builder, and another junior cook to the dungeon on Tuesday.

He sent his electrician, two servants, and his music instructor to the dungeon on Thursday.

On Wednesday, he did not send anybody because he was busy opening a new Tesco store.

On Friday, he was in a foul mood, so poor that he got the medication ill. Seven of his staff were hauled down the dirty stairs at the castle's base and dumped into the dungeon's black pit.

On Saturday, there were two more, but there was only one since the King spent most of the day at prayer on Sunday.

On Monday morning, the king awoke in his dim bedroom and reached out to ring the bell for a worker.

Before raising the curtains, the servant bowed and said, "Good morning, your Majesty."

The king never said good morning to someone before ordering his tea.

The servant began to quake with fear; in truth, he shook so hard that he couldn't talk.

"What's the problem?" The king roared. The servant, on the other hand, could only stand and turn.

Down TO THE DUNGEON! The king yelled, enraged at being represented by such a moron.

However, no guards arrived this time, even though the king had gotten out of bed in his pajamas and screamed down the hallway once more.

The   servant   shook   his   head   and   stutteringly stutteringlystutteringlystutteringlystutteringlystutteringly stuttering

There are no guards, and there is no breakfast, your majesty.

It was excessive. The King drew himself up to his maximum height and took such a deep breath that the queen feared he might burst.

What, no breakfast? There are no security guards? He screamed. Where in the hell are they?

Even if he was already sweating like a foolish double jelly, the servant managed to whisper, All in the cellar, your majesty, where you sent them.

The king blinked, then blinked again, then, believe it or not, he blinked a third time!

The queen sneered, "It's real." You've been going insane all week.

The king couldn't live without his servants, guards, or breakfast.

So we'd best get them out of the cellar, he shouted and sent his servant to order the dungeon keeper to let them out of the dirty stairs' dark pit.

But the stairs were no longer dirty, and the dark hole was no longer a black hole.

The king's electrician had installed lighting in the dungeon. The plumber had prevented the water from pouring down the walls. The rats had relocated to another dungeon that was already damp and dark. The gardener was raising cabbages and other lovely vegetables alongside the mushrooms.

The music instructor had taken down his stereo, the chefs had set up a kitchen and were preparing delectable meals, and the designer had brightened up the room by painting the walls in vibrant colors.

As the servant returned to the king's bedroom, he had been trembling so badly that he had run out of shake and remained perfectly still in front of the King.

Your Majesty, the servant, was now at ease. Your servants and guards will not be returning.

The king turned to face the emperor, and the queen turned to face the king. They had never before been disobeyed.

The king cried, "Guard!" The queen covered her eyes; the king was silly once again, and no guards were there.

The king screamed, "I'll resolve this!" He marched down the sterile stairs to the basement, his crown tight on his head and his silk robe wrapped around him.

He could hear the music and smell the breakfast frying before he even got to the bottom. His servants and guards were tucking into stacks of sausages, chickens, pork, and beans in the cellar. The sight of too much food made the King's mouth water, and his hunger grows stronger.

Please get me some breakfast! He yelled.

Shant, his plumber, said. The gardener declared, "It's ours."

The king was at a loss about what to do; no one was paying attention to him.

He pleaded softly, "Please?"

All put down their forks. Please, the King had asked! For the first time in history.

The plumber bent over and slapped two large sausages, a rasher of bacon, and some beans onto the pan.

The plumber snapped, "You're not having an eggy, and you don't need one."

Might I please get eggy?

Everyone was staring at this point. The king had requested twice!

When are you going and return to look after me? The king was challenging to comprehend since he spoke while holding two sausages in his mouth, somewhat impolite.

All of the guards and servants yelled, "We're not going back!"

There's no point; you're such a jerk that you keep sending us to the dungeon.

Assume I double your salary. The king said.

All put down their forks.

Then grab those happy pills. The plumber demanded.

Often, every week, send us a day off. The gardener said.

And allows us to flip on the television. The electrician sobbed.

The King fought valiantly. He was tired of being grumpy and thought it would be a good thing to be joyful for a change.

As a result, the king nodded. And everybody applauded and tossed their sausages in the air with joy.

Just one more thing! A woman from the rear rang out.

What is that, the King inquired?

That you allowed us to stay in the dungeon, the voice screamed. And it's so warm in here right now.

Of necessity, the king was delighted to consent.

The Wife of the Wizard

There was once upon a time when there was a Wizard. He was a very nice Wizard; in particular, he was an extremely nice Wizard. The Wizard was married to a lovely woman, but she was just sweet, not extremely nice like the Wizard.

She wasn't polite, and she was always asking the Wizard what to do.

Have you finished the prime minister's miracle cocktail yet? Have you purchased some more frog tails for the circus clown's spell? What for the zoo visitors' forest juice?

And so it continued, day after day, day after day, until the Wizard was fully drained.

He expressed his undying affection for his child. But there are days that I wish she will be silent for a few moments.

You are a wizard! Have you created the underground broth for the mysterious people who dwell in the mysterious cave?

His wife was gone once more, barking orders at him as he worked in his magical blending area.

The hidden broth was a broth crafted of secret ingredients that were so well-kept that even the Wizard had little idea what the secret people did with it. What he understood was that it had to be done carefully.

He began by taking a large carrot and carefully shredding it before adding it to a pot of boiling water that had gone wrong.

Don't ask me what a pot of boiling water gone bad is because I have no idea – I'm not a Wizard.

Then he added the next hidden ingredient and stirred it into the bath. Don't ask me what the hidden ingredient was because, once again, I have no idea; I'm only telling you the story.

The Wizard climbed to the peak of one of his dusty shelves and lowered a tiny stone bottle with a strong screw top. It was the final component of the hidden both!

You are a wizard! His wife's crying sound drifted into his mixing area. The Wizard sighed when his wife began to speak again.

Don't forget to mix some paint to polish the engine, and keep in mind that Mrs. Smith is always waiting for some stardust, and when you're finished, give me a cup of tea.

Wearily, the Wizard opened his stardust cabinet and spooned a teaspoonful of the shiny dust into a little envelope labeled 'FOR MRS SMITH.' Another ten minutes of intense stirring was needed to blend the car polish, and by the time he finished making the tea, the mystery people were banging on the door for their secret soup.

Three smiles and a handshake said the Wizard as he handed over the secret broth.

People in Wizard land don't have money; they pay for stuff by smiling and shaking each other's hands. A package of wriggly chocolates will cost you twenty smiles, two handshakes, and a tickle on the bottom!

The Wizard was sipping his tea calmly when Boom, BANG, BANG!

Someone was banging so loudly that the Wizard felt his door might open!

I want to reclaim my smiles and my handshake! Before the magician could even raise his mouth, the secret figure was screaming on the doorstep.

This isn't hidden broth; the secret guy was irritated. He was jumping up and down in anger. It's just carrot soup!

An unknown person slammed down the bottle.

You can almost taste it.

The Wizard had no idea what the secret broth was like, but when he sipped a spoonful from the glass, he knew he was drinking carrot soup.

He paused with a gasp as he rushed back into his mixing area. His mixing table already had the stone bottle with the strong screw top!

He had completely neglected to have it in the hidden broth for the secret citizens!

He returned the container to the hidden individual after quickly dumping it into the secret broth.

I'm so sorry, he sobbed, but my wife keeps talking to me, and I'm missing things!

That's extremely risky, said the unknown male. Particularly while concocting magical concoctions.

The Wizard had no choice but to consent, and after the magic guy had left, he sat down on his sofa for a long, hard thought.

We all knew he adored his mom, but her constant chatter and interruptions were causing him to make mistakes.

He did have a mystical charm that would stop her from communicating, but if he used it, she would never be able to speak again, which was much too cruel to do to someone.

So, all night, he rummaged through his large books of spells and potions, hoping to locate anything that might save his wife from constantly interrupting him. But no matter how closely he looked or scanned his books from cover to cover, nothing in the realm of magic could support him.

The next day in the magical land playground, he asked the elf who pulled the enchanted swings for people to assist.

The little elf suggested that you make her into a block of stone.

"I don't have that much strength," the Wizard said, "I can only create potions and cast spells." "Can't you make a potion that transforms her into a block of stone?" the elf inquired. The Wizard made a shaky motion of his head.

There isn't a potion to achieve so, he lamented.

You are a wizard!

The wizard frowned while his wife resumed her work.

Tomorrow, you must cast three spells: one for the pumpkin guy, one for the woman who smiles upside down, and one for the spider who has forgotten how to spin a web.

The Wizard crept out of the back door quietly and cautiously along the garden road. He went to the three witches' square in the village center.

He still went there when he was tired, and seeing the witches boil mystical vegetables in their cauldrons over blazing flames and smelling the tasty meals they prepared made him feel a lot better.

He was seated on a bench under a lamppost when his pointed cap abruptly bent sideways!

Taking it off, he exclaimed in horror; YUCK! was written all down the side of his pointed cap! Yucky bird! A pigeon had pooh-poohed the magician. Since birds in magical land will laugh, the bird flew away laughing.

The Wizard took out his magical handkerchief and watched it clean his cap. Instead of being irritated, he was starting to get an idea.

Slowly, he started his walk home, his idea becoming clearer and clearer as he marched faster and faster until, by the time he arrived at his door, he was running like hell.

He dashed into his mixing area, grabbed his book of spells, and began flipping through it.

Laughter! He exclaimed triumphantly.

What have you been up to? What about the charms, and there are two more... The Wizard's wife flailed her mouth once more, but instead of responding, the Wizard's arms began to wave in a spellbinding manner. His whole hand was pointed at his wife's forehead, and he was singing phrases she had never heard before.

His body started to stretch, becoming larger and longer as he became bigger and taller.

Mrs. Wizard has never seen anything like it before! As the Wizard grew in size, she backed out of the room, terrified.

The Wizard, on the other hand, was not growing any bigger!

Mrs. Wizard has no idea that the reason the Wizard now seemed so large was that Mrs. Wizard was becoming smaller and smaller! If she had looked down, she might have seen that her feet had transformed into long nails, her arms had transformed into wings, and her whole body was coated with feathers!

His companion had been transformed into a bird by the Wizard! Climbing the stairs to his attic, the Wizard rummaged through dusty and cobweb-infested crates before, with a triumphant cackle, he pulled out a huge birdcage that he had purchased years ago but had neglected to fill with a bird.

Mrs Wizard was also unaware that she had been transformed into a bird, so she was taken aback when the Wizard picked her up and put her in his large birdcage.

What about the charms, and there are two more... She cackled once more but was abruptly silenced when a cover was thrown over the cage.

The Wizard leaned back in his chair, relaxed.

Changing his wife into a bird was a good idea, but changing her into a parrot was much better; now, he could always speak to his wife anytime he needed to, and if she reminded him, he could shut her up by covering her. With a blanket! He wouldn't have to purchase her any more dresses, shoes, or fish and chips. He might have her birdseed for a lot less money.

And then the Wizard and his parrot companion lived happily ever after, and the parrot wife lived happily ever after because parrots don't have to do the dishes or housework!

Bendy

Bendy was a guy who lived once upon a time. Bendy got his nickname because he was still hunched over, his face a couple of inches off the ground as he shuffled along, as though he was searching for something.

This was about right, given that he WAS still searching for something. It was mostly a bit of string, an empty sweet bag, or an old newspaper that had been dropped.

He still took a large plastic carry bag with him as he went out, and he would throw anything he found in it.

When he got home, the bag was so full that it took a huge push and a lot of huffing and puffing to get it through his door. But the bag was frequently clean, and all he noticed was in his pockets.

You're still curious about what Bendy did about everything he discovered. If I told you that every space in Bendy's house was crammed full of plastic bags, you'd understand that Bendy never threw everything he noticed out because, in certain areas of his house, Bendy had to squeeze sideways to get around all the bulging plastic bags.

When he came home with not one but two plastic bags, the trouble began. He had begun with one but had discovered so much trash that this bag was easily filled; luckily, amid the debris blowing down the road was another plastic bag. Bendy pursued it, which is difficult when the nose is just a few inches off the ice!

After capturing the bag, he loaded it with trash, and, as I previously said, the trouble began when he attempted to enter his front door.

Bendy couldn't get through the door because it was just a little too small.

The door will not open anymore, no matter how far he pressed. Bendy stood on the doorstep, thinking deeply. What do you do when you are unable to open a door? Bendy had no idea, and he had never had a door that did not open before.

But, what's the big deal? The voice boomed out, deep and clear.

When Bendy glanced around, he saw a police officer looking down at him.

Bendy explained his dilemma and pulled and heaved against the door with the policeman.

Police officers are very strong; otherwise, they might not be police officers, yet still, the officer could not move the lock with all of his strength.

Call the council! Exclaimed the cop. They are excellent at opening frames.

The councilman entered easily and, after a short shove, realized something was wrong right away.

He mentioned that there are so many plastic bags in your corridor. Any of them must be relocated.

The councilman summoned a garbage truck and extracted some of the plastic sacks with the assistance of the dustmen, and then they extracted even more, and even more, and still more!

The councilman was taken aback because he had never seen so many plastic bags in his life!

However, the door finally unlocked sufficiently for the councilman to enter the building.

The guy from the council almost popped to pieces in surprise, his head sticking around the door and his hand clutching more plastic bags.

There were plastic bags, more plastic bags, and still more plastic bags along the corridor, in all the doorways, up the stairs, and along the landing. The bags were stacked so tightly that they were almost breaking from floor to ceiling, from outlets to walls.

The councilman yelled into his phone, "Help!" No, no, no, no, no, no, no, no, no, no No way! We have a major concern here with seven garbage lorries.

Bendy stood in his front yard, watching as gangs of staff removed his prized plastic bags. Tears welled up in his eyes as each lorry departed, loaded down with all his lovely garbage, and by the time the last lorry left, he was sobbing pitifully.

He went into his house after the councilman and the lorries had gone. It was exactly as it had been when he began collecting garbage. He saw tables and benches he hadn't seen in months and stepped on the carpet for the first time since New Year's.

He might finally take a bath, watch TV, and listen to the radio since they had both been buried by plastic bags.

He could cook on his stove, use the laundry machine, and even look out the walls.

You'd assume he'd be relieved to get all of his things returned, but he wasn't. Not at all, and that night he said himself, "I'm going to start searching for garbage again tomorrow."

He noticed an empty beer can, a water container, and a hamburger wrapper within five minutes the next morning. Feeling far better, he stuffed the litter into his pants, vowing to locate a plastic bin.

So who was obstructing his progress? The member of the assembly.

Bendy! You've done it once again!

Bendy felt very sorry, as he could after causing too many problems with the council.

Observing Bendy's cheerful smile, The councilman realized Bemdy was never comfortable until he was gathering trash.

On the other hand, the council does not afford to vacuum Bendy's house every few weeks.

Come along with me. Bendy was followed by a councilman into the council depot and then into the large building behind the town hall.

Take a look at Bendy. The councilman flung open one of the massive gates.

Bendy exclaimed. Bendy opened his eyes and blinked. Bendy shook with ecstasy. Garbage was strewn around the length of the massive structure in front of him, in masses, piles, mounds, and valleys.

When Bendy was staring, the door at the other end of the building opened, and a dustcart backed in, tipped its back, and dumped in another ton of garbage.

How would you like to work as a garbage collector?

Bendy was taken aback at the prospect of such a great career. He couldn't help but smile.

So Bendy became a street sweeper, picking trash every day and having a great time doing it.

And the best part was that he was being compensated for it.

Bendy gladly served with the council for the rest of his life, and the council breathed a sigh of relaxation that they no longer had to clear out Bendy's home!

The One Who Couldn't Stop Snoring.

Once upon a time, there was an elderly guy who would head to the nearby park for a nap every day. A nap is much less than a wink, but the older man slept for longer than a nap because he would have gone to the park for a snooze.

But while the older man slept, he snored; he snored so heavily that the children who were playing ball on the lawn could hear him.

Some people said the older man was a witch, but Little Charlie had been to the park often and had never seen the older man cast any spells or do any magic tricks.

It was also great fun for the kids to circle the older man as he puffed and flapped while snoring.

He puffed as he inhaled deeply and flapped his mouth as he exhaled deeply. Often it was just a snore, and on other occasions, oh my god, the disturbance was so loud it felt like a train was approaching!

The girls, of course, laughed, and when he snored extra loudly, some of them collapsed to the deck, weak from laughter. But when he snored extra loudly, some of the kids found it so amusing that they collapsed on their backs and waved their legs in the breeze!

Little Charlie, who was little, which is why he was nicknamed Little Charlie, would press his way to the front so that he could not only see the man's nose wiggle as he breathed in and his lips flapping as he breathed out, but if it was a bright day, he could also see the man's tonsils jumping!

A big wasp appeared on the man's nose one day when he made the man's tonsil dance up and down while the other children were all on their backs throwing their legs in the breeze.

With a massive snore, the guy not only drew in a huge wave of dirt, but he even pulled off the wasp's yellow and black stripes! The wasp, shocked at being undressed in such a way, flew away in fear, fearful that the older man would suck its legs off as well.

Then the unthinkable occurred!

The older man snored loudly, and Little Charlie, who sat directly in front of him, was covered in the yellow and black wasp stripes!

It was too much for the other kids, who couldn't stop laughing and waving their legs in the air as they noticed Little Charlie's face coated in stripes. They did something heinous so that they couldn't save themselves. They were all drenched!

Little Charlie was still smiling, which made the other kids laugh even more because Little Charlie had no idea he was coated in stripes!

When he returned home, though, his mother did not joke.

She yelled, "Wash those stupid stripes off right now!"

But ten minutes later, as Little Charlie emerged from the bathroom still coated with wasp streaks, his mother took a large sponge, placed Little Charlie in the large sink, and began scrubbing.

The stripes failed to budge no matter how vigorously she scrubbed, and even when Little Charlie's father came home and tried a tube of special stripe remover, Little Charlie went to bed with a yellow and black striped face.

When Little Charlie's classmates noticed him, they all burst out laughing, and even the teachers had to smile.

The yellow and black stripes resisted any efforts by physicians and clinics to fade them even slightly with various drugs and creams, and Little Charlie's clarification as to how they fell on his face just made people laugh even more.

Then something odd happened one day.

A wasp fell on Charlie's nose!

The wasp stuck up its little front legs and shook its little head so he could shake it off since wasps bite humans.

Little Charlie squinted, having never seen a wasp behaving like that before. The wasp then took off, flying in front of him towards the front door.

It took three tries for the wasp to convince Little Charlie that the wasp needed him to pursue it.

The wasp buzzed out the front door and led Little Charlie down the street, around the corner, and into the park.

The regular audience of smiling children gathered around the seat to hear the old man snore was there. The wasp swooped through the children and settled on the seat next to the elderly gentleman. Charlie led the children's legs on his hands and knees until he was seated in front of the older man.

Getting too near to the snores was incredibly loud and draughty, and little Charlie wondered what he was doing there.

The wasp, though, took flight and began buzzing furiously in circles about the old guy.

Little Charlie saw a black object arrive; it was the same size as the wasp and moved in a circle with it for the time being.

Charlie, the little boy, wiped his eyes. It was a wasp that didn't have any stripes! It was the wasp that had given Little Charlie its stripes!

The wasp with the stripes abruptly ascended high over the old guy, hovered for a second, then dived down and landed on Little Charlie's stomach, much to Little Charlie's horror.

But instead of a bite, Little Charlie felt a kick when the wasp forced him to step closer to the old guy.

When Charlie was just a few centimeters away from the older man's nose, he heaved his chest and inhaled a massive lungful of breath, causing the breeze to blow through Little Charlie's head.

At the precise moment, a wasp with no stripes appeared on Little Charlie's nose! Little Charlie now had a wasp in front of him and another in the back!

The older man snuffled for a second, then breathed out his chest full of air all over Little Charlie and the wasps with a mighty snore and his lips flapping like two pancakes.

Little Charlie stared in awe as the back wasp on his nose brightened up. Stripes of yellow and black flew out of the older man's mouth and wound themselves around its neck!

For the first time, the children were not waving their legs in the air in response to the man's extra-loud snore; instead, they were staring at Little Charlie with a strange expression.

Little Charlie did not like it when people looked at him strangely, so he immediately squeezed his way out of the crowd of children and returned home.

His mother even stared at him curiously in the house, and his father came up too close to gaze at him in the garden that Little Charlie could see his tonsils.

His father ran his fingertips across Little Charlie's face slowly.

They've vanished! He sobbed. The stripes are no longer visible!

Charlie dashed into the bathroom and examined himself in the mirror. His profile, normal and devoid of any striations, returned his grin.

He hadn't realized how sad the wasp would have been to sacrifice its stripes because he was thinking about seeing the wasp's stripes all over his forehead.

The wasps, unlike his mother and father, the physicians, the ambulance, and all the creams and remedies they had tried, understood just what had happened.

The older man truly had a mystical snore, and it was only by returning to the magical snore that they were able to return the stripes to their proper place.

That made the wasps smarter than Little Charlie, his mother and father, the physicians, and the hospital.

Jemima

Jemima grew up in the country on a large farm with many livestock. Some pigs still kept their snouts in the trough and took no heed of Jemima as she talked to them, only snorting and chewing.

The chickens stayed beside the large farmhouse; they were constantly clucking and scraping among themselves and were much too preoccupied to mess with any other livestock.

The sheep were nosy, rushing up to her as Jemima approached but then fleeing almost as soon when they saw she didn't have enough for them.

We won't even bring up the pigs. They will smile at Jemima and, with a haughty grin, toss their heads in the air, then turn their backs and stalk away.

Even the cows were snobbish, which was shocking because they were part of her kin, as Jemima was one of them; in truth, Jemima was a cow.

The only thing that had the animals all going was blackberries. Three days a week, the farmer would carry large buckets of blackberries for his livestock because he cherished them all and decided to feed them.

So it came as a disappointment when the farmer appeared one day with just half a bucketful of berries.

He yelled, "That's what there is, animals!" The animals have devoured the majority!

The scramble for the berries was terrible; the goats shoved everyone else away to get to the bucket, while the sheep, who were a little slower, but the goats' back legs to get them out of the way. The pigs snorted and charged at each other. The sheep and Jemima's kin were forced and shoved their way into the battle for the berries.

Jemima, who was much more polite than the others, discovered nothing when she arrived at the bucket; all the berries had vanished!

The animals grumbled among themselves about the birds consuming the berries, but when Jemima informed them about her plan, they simply turned their backs and walked away.

We should build a scarecrow! Jemima had yelled out loudly, overjoyed by her brilliant concept.

Jemima soon realized that if they wanted to save the birds from consuming the berries, she would have to create the scarecrow herself.

She searched the old barn for a pitchfork, an old overcoat, some straw, and an old hat and produced a very, very good-looking scarecrow with her teeth.

She carefully planted the scarecrow in the field that evening, right next to the bushes where the berries rose.

She crawled into the field quite early the next morning, then froze in astonishment, her mouth wide open and her horns quivering.

Not only were the birds already chewing the fruit, but two of them were perched on the scarecrow!

These birds were either very naive because they didn't realize the scarecrow was there to scare them or very smart because they realized it wasn't an actual human and wouldn't hurt them. But it didn't matter since the birds were already consuming the animal's blackberries, smart or lazy.

The sheep smiled, and even the pigs stopped snorting to smile— what a squandering of time. Scarecrows are no longer working here.

Jemima mooed loudly in disgust and marched aggressively back to the old stable, snatching the scarecrow in her hands.

When Jemima did not return to bed that night, the cow family was taken aback. And she hadn't returned the next morning, so she skipped breakfast.

But there was a new scarecrow in the field with the berries, far larger than the last one, and things were quite different this time.

The birds landed at the crack of dawn and made directly for their perch on the scarecrow's shoulders.

MOOOOOOOOOOOOOOOOOOOOOOOOOOOOOOOOOOOOOOO

The squawks of fear, the flapping of wings, and the sky

darkening as it filled with terrified birds battling to get away from the mooing scarecrow drew all the animals to the area.

MOOOOOOOOOOOOOOOOOOOOOOOOOOOOOOOOOOOOOOO

The scarecrow is now flapping its arms and shaking its head! The last two birds flew away like missiles, one of the pigs hid behind the dogs, and the hens were so amused that they raced around in circles pecking each other on the bottom!

The scarecrow then removed its hat, much to the animal's surprise!

The goats yanked on their beards, their eyes dancing in surprise. There was ahead under the cap. And the head belonged to somebody they were both familiar with.

And then someone in question was Jemima!

The sound of all the animals clapping in the excitement caused the birds who consumed the berries to flee evermore. Both of the animals kissed Jemima on the back to express their gratitude for saving their berries before returning to their fields arm in arm to continue eating the grass.

Please be patient! Jemima moaned. Where do you believe you're going?

The livestock came to a halt. They both said, "We're going to get some pancakes!"

Who will be the next scarecrow? Jemima demanded. The birds will return if we leave the berries unguarded.

The animals stared in shock at Jemima, perplexed as to how someone might be so astute as to conceive about such a brilliant idea.

I'm not going to be a dumb scarecrow, a pig snorted. "And stand in the field like an idiot pig all day. "Then you won't be able to eat any of the berries that we spare, said Jemima.

The animals pondered for a long time, muttering to one another and peering between the berries and Jemima.

OK, shuffled one of the sheep away; I'll be the scarecrow today.

And tomorrow I'll be the scarecrow. A big hen nodded and fluttered her wings.

So, each day, a new animal dressed up as a scarecrow and either snorted, clucked, mooed, or bathed when the birds approached the berry bushes.

About a week, the farmer returned with three large buckets of berries for the animals to feast on, and all of the animals concluded that the berries were twice as good as before because the birds no longer pecked them, and also that the animals had done this together for the first time! Anything on the farm became twice as special as a result!

Ozzy Zebra

Mary was a zebra that lived in Africa amid a large group of zebras, but Mary was the most excited of the bunch.

What was she so excited about?

That she was going to have a kid the following day!

The baby zebra was called Ozzy because Ozzy the zebra seemed way nicer and stronger than the names of other newborn zebra infants, Zara, Zizi, and Zozo.

At two o'clock in the afternoon, the young little zebra gave two skips of joy at entering the universe.

Mary boldly leads her baby out of her hut the next morning to introduce it to the rest of the herd.

She stepped in front, her head raised high, with Ozzie running along behind her. However, as she passed, the other zebras turned to look at Ozzie. The zebras whispered to each other and shared confused looks as frowns spread across the herd.

Ozzie was strange.

They couldn't figure out what was different about him, so he wasn't like the rest of the herd.

Ozzie's father sobbed, "He's not like the rest of us."

Any member of the herd circled little Ozzie, inspecting him from his ears to his hooves. He walked like the others; he had black and white lines like the others, he had ears, a nose, eyes, and a head like the others, but something wasn't quite right.

Stop it, Ozzie's mother yelled. Even, please leave my little boy alone!

The herd was led by an elderly zebra with knobbly feet, a knobbly head, and a knobbly tail. After learning that there was a zebra in the pack that was not exactly like the others, he became concerned.

If a Zebra differed from the rest, it would be forced to abandon the herd.

He directed that Ozzie be brought before him.

Ozzie stared into the eyes of the herd's leader, and the herd's leader felt his heartbreak at the sight of such a beautiful little zebra.

HA! The howl erupted from behind the herd's back.

HOW OUT OF THEIR MINDS!

All turned to look at the herd's wife's head.

If the herdsman had knobbly knees, a knobbly head, and a knobbly tail, the herdsman's wife had knobbly knees, a knobbly head, and a knobbly tail.

WHAT A HASSLE! The wife of the herd's leader was smiling at Ozzie.

Look at the black and white streaks on his sleeve! She let out a snort.

Now, the herd's leader wasn't just the herd's leader for no reason. Now that his wife had figured out little Ozzie's black and white markings, it was clear to him, if not to the other zebras, why little Ozzie seemed so odd.

His stripes are running in the wrong direction! Exclaimed his mom. Our stripes go all the way up and down our legs.

It was right! Little Ozzie's markings ran in straight lines around his fur.

He must abandon the herd! The herd's leader was heartbroken to accept that because he adored Ozzie, but laws were rules and could not be broken.

But if he's left alone, he'll die, sobbed his mum. That night, the last night Little Ozzie will be able to remain with his mother and aunt, was so emotional that the family almost burst into tears.

But, just as the new day began, Ozzie's father quit weeping because he had an idea! He went down to the valley on the other side of the river, taking Ozzie with him. There was a large tree in the valley that was coated in large black spheres.

Ozzie's father struck the tree trunk with his head, causing some of the large black balls to fall to the ground with a sharp thwack. The fall had broken them apart, and black liquid spilled out of the balls, creating a large puddle under the tree.

Bring it on! Ozzie's father was given the order. Ozzie didn't need to be told twice and gladly rolled in the black pool until he was fully wrapped in the black substance from head to tail. Ozzie was now totally black, like a black horse rather than a zebra.

Then his father trotted over to another oak. The balls on the tree were white this time, and after Ozzie's father shaken the tree, there was another pool under the tree, except this time it was white.

Ozzie's father softly rolled his son in the white puddle, but just once on either foot, and as Ozzie stood up, the white substance streaked down the sides of his neck, bringing him...

I'm sure you guessed it – white lines that went up and down!

Ozzie now resembled the other zebras!

When his father took him back to the herd, his mother turned over on her back in delight. Ozzie will now continue with the herd!

The other zebras no longer saw Ozzie, and why should they be? He resembled the other teenage zebras, Zara, Zizi, and Zozo.

Now, the leader of the herd's wife would often travel around the herd and ensure that all the zebras were acting properly.

Where did you have your baby zebra? She inquired of Ozzie's mother.

But it's Ozzie, his mother neighed. Have you seen how his stripes have changed?

The wife of the herd's leader was dubious. Even a zebra named Ozzie can't change his stripes.

Suddenly, she picked up a bucket of water between her teeth and hurled it at Ozzie with a huge swing of her head!

The poor zebra was almost soaked! Worse, the liquid from the black and white fruit was drained out as the water cascaded down his body.

Every zebra exclaimed. Ozzie's stripes have flipped upside down!

FRAUD! The wife yelled. IMMEDIATELY LEAVE THE HERD!

What is going on here? The herd's leader is knobbly on his knobbly feet. When he met young Ozzie, he realized what had happened. Although, as we all know, the herd's leader was not just the herd's leader for no reason; behind his knobbly appearance, he was a rather clever animal.

He needed to think quickly because he didn't want little Ozzie to be kicked out of the herd.

Fantastic! He screamed, "A zebra with horizontal lines!"

His wife and the herd stared at him, wondering if their leader had gone insane.

That's just what I needed!

The herd's leader was now the only zebra who could write. Since there wasn't a lot of paper to write on in Africa, the herd's leader often had to wait days until anyone came along with any paper.

He could now compose his letters on Little Ozzie's row! And this is what caused both of the zebras to stand on their hind legs and clap their hooves together. Ozzie, the little dog, may bring the message!

And the head of the herd's wife had to admit that they were fortunate to have little Ozzie, and everybody hoped that Ozzie's mother might have more little zebras with horizontal stripes so that the head of the herd could write a book one day!

The Broken-Wanded Fairy

CRACKLE!

Elvie, the fairy, looked horrified.

The small goldenrod with the glittering star on top was broken and lying on the floor in two parts.

Oh, my God! Elvie exclaimed. My magic wand!

A fairy's most valuable possession is her wand; without it, she cannot perform magic or cast spells since it is the wand when she taps the individual or object that causes the magic and spells to function.

Elvie's wand was shattered on the concrete.

She gently picked up the top piece and studied it.

Maybe it always functions, she said to herself. She discovered a basic spell when she opened her fairy iPad, which held all of her spells.

She whispered the magic spell while tapping her wand on her seat.

I'll see what happens at this table—a sweet, hot, steaming cup of tea.

When she tapped the table, the normal beam of light and cloud of smoke occurred as the magic activated.

Elvie was glad at first, but when the smoke settled, her joy changed to horror. There was a great big guy on the table instead of a nice cup of tea!

Elvie gazed, astounded, and the guy, judging from his look, was astounded as well.

Where am I? enquired the guy. I enjoyed a cup of tea in a café when it all went dark, and I found myself here.

Elvie thought rapidly as she glanced at her missing wand. It was clear that it wasn't running properly.

What is your given name? She inquired of the man.

Mr. Leigh, he responded, always stunned.

In frustration, Elvie smacked her forehead with her fist.

Cup of tea, Mr. Leigh – they rhyme! She exclaimed. Her faulty wand had messed up the spell. It had given a Mr. Leigh instead of a cup of tea!

Elvie gently picked the lower half of her wand and Sellotape the two halves together after giving Mr. Leigh his bus fare back to the café.

Now it would work; she smiled and opened her fairy iPad to find another spell, this time a straightforward one that would not trigger any trouble.

She chanted the second spell in the book while waving her wand in the breeze.

Bring me a lovely flower with your strength, my wand.

She motioned with her wand.

THUNDER! BANG! WHACK! WHACK!

The echo was deafening! Great clouds of dust billowed around her, and the wall of her house collapsed in another massive smash. There was a huge thump, the earth rocked, and everything went black.

Elvie peered around the space as the dense dust cleared, wiping herself off and hacking like a cough drop.

Her fairy hair was standing on end, and her mouth was open so big that her head jumped on the cement!

A massive tower stood in her front room, the walls vanishing into her ceiling.

The fractured wand had screwed up once again, moving from flower to tower.

It can't sit there forever! Elvie sobbed. I can't deal with a large tower in my living space.

It took some digging to locate the next spell Elvie desired, but at the end of her spell list, the solution to her dilemma flashed on the page.

Elvie chanted her spell while carefully properly waving her arms so that there will be no more errors.

This tower is causing a lot of problems; please get rid of it as soon as possible!

When you expect somebody to do something at the double, you ask them to do so really quickly. And Elvie was in a hurry to get the tower down.

THUNDER! BANG! WHACK! WHACK! Elvie's jaw fell open far more comprehensive than before when the dust billowed in, and the earth rocked, and when the dust cleared, her chin rolled twice on the carpet.

There's something I haven't taught you about the term double, and I doubt Elvie is aware of it either. The term "double" implies not only "fast" but also "two."

Yes, you guessed correctly. Elvie now had two towers since the dust settled!

She sighed when she said no. I can't keep on like this; my wand is destroying everything!

When fairies have issues, which isn't always since they have so much magic, only one individual can help. - the neighborhood magician

The wizard frowned and shook his wise old head, holding a bit of the shattered wand in each palm. Fairies...wrong charms, spilled fairy dust, jumping all night, and waking neighbors were all things he was used to, except suddenly they were breaking their wands.

Elvie explained, "I sat on it."

The Wizard repeated, "You sat on it." He snarled, "You're a silly fairy." And you're much more delusory if you believe I should fix it.

Elvie was taken aback by the wizard's abilities; wizards could do something.

According to your fairy instruction guide, the only one that can mend a bent wand is the fairy herself.

Elvie stared at the magician, wide-eyed since she'd never bothered to read the fairy wand guidance guide.

That night, in bed with a steaming cup of fairy hot cocoa, she read the fairy guidance book slowly and carefully.

There were cleaning orders, but she had never followed them. There were directions about how to wave it; she waved it as she pleased, only counting the right amount of waves needed for the casting spell. There were even directions for where to store it while she wasn't using it. The warning 'never leave your wand on a chair, you could sit on it' was highlighted in red. That's just what she'd achieved!

She searched for the last tab, right at the bottom, below the directions on how to locate a missing wand.

HOW TO REPAIR A WAND AFTER SITTING ON IT

It said she had to go back to the wizard and have him slap her ass for being such a naughty fairy for not being vigilant and not looking where she sat, and then she had to cast a spell.

She had to wave the magic design with her hands because she couldn't use the wand, so first, she had to make sure her hands were spotless.

I'm not going to be smacked on the butt by the wizard! She sobbed. And I'm too lazy to wash my face!

You must go, my wand, to the mender in the clouds. The wand vanished with a cloud of smoke and a burst of light. Elvie, relieved that a spell was finally functioning, waited the five minutes specified in the directions before chanting the final spell.

a component of the spell

When you've repaired yourself, just tap, tap on my side.

Elvis heard, but no one knocked on her threshold. She sat on a chair behind the door all day in case she lost her wand ticking.

Unfortunately, as she reached the stairs that night, her wand had not returned; maybe it couldn't be fixed, perhaps it had gotten misplaced in the fairy box, maybe... All she realized was that she couldn't continue to be a fairy without a wand. Without one, spells and sorcery will be useless.

Tears streamed down her cheeks as she sobbed herself to sleep late at night.

Her fairy Phone jolted her awake. It was the wizard's note. She needed to see him right then.

Just show me your hands! He screamed as soon as she stepped into his cave. Elvis pushed two filthy hands forward.

It's disgusting! The magician slapped his stick on the head of a frog on which he was casting a spell, causing its eyes to squint.

The wizard's wand mender, the wizard, bonked the frog again, causing it to burp. You haven't come here for a playful smack, which tells me you haven't been here for a playful smack.

Elvis closed her eyes and shook her head; she'd been naughty twice so, and it was really serious.

Get on your knees! Waving his stick in the breeze, the wizard gave the order. Elvis grasped the table's edge and watched.

The wizard swung his stick down on Elvis' butt with a swish, the smack cracked, and dust rose from her fairy skirts.

One point for not showing up for the slap. The magician lifted his stick once more, this time with a swish and a SMACK! The stick kicked up still more dust from Elvie's feet.

You get two points for not washing your face! It had not been completed. For the third cycle, the magician wound himself up.

There are three! "A slap for not being careful where you rest." The final smack was the most strong, bringing tears to the wizard's eyes.

Elvie walked quietly around, knowing that by not performing what she was instructed, she had received three smacks instead of one and that she had been very, very naughty.

She would be more cautious about where she stood in the future, wash her face, and still do what she was advised.

She enjoyed a cup of butterfly tea in her fairy kitchen when she noticed a knock on the threshold.

ENTIRELY!

She yanked the door open, giddy with joy, and there, leaning against the doorpost, was her wand, all in one piece!

She gently picked it up and placed it in its case for safety.

Oh, I almost forgot! She waved her arms in the air and stared up at the ceiling.

Now that it's all finished and done with, I'm undoing my previous spell.

Elvie's bottom rattled twice after a loud ping.

Fairies are not stupid; they realize that their bottoms will get smacked, but they do something really clever: they cast a spell that makes them experience nothing when the stick touches their feet!

A Penny and a Pound

A woman had a purse, a large purse that contained all the money she had in her pocket, filled with coins and banknotes jumbled together, bulging like a fat man's chest.

When the woman opened the purse and let in the draught, the coins and banknotes were overjoyed to be so close together; they could joke and cuddle up close to each other.

They were content until the woman went shopping, at which point the coins and banknotes realized they were about to miss any of their mates.

If the woman went into a little store, they could miss a couple of coins, but if she went into a major shop, AY, AY, AY, AY, AY, AY, AY! That was serious; they could lose some of the banknotes!

Banknotes were more valuable than coins since they were more expensive.

A five-penny coin told a ten-penny coin that there were five hundred ten-penny coins rolled up in a five-pound note; the queen's eyes on the ten-penny coin widened in amazement, and she couldn't sleep for a week because she was so taken aback.

The fifty-pound note was, of course, the most valuable currency, but they were very scarce, and none of the coins or notes had ever seen one.

The five-penny coin would have had a fit and spun itself silly if it had told the ten-penny coin how many five-penny coins were in the fifty-pound bill.

Because, since the coins in the woman's pocket had never seen a fifty-pound bill, the ten-penny coin didn't need to tell something.

The snobbish one-pound coins held to themselves in one section of the pouch, thinking their sweet yellow colour was much superior to the other coins' silver and copper colours.

There was a five-pound note, all blue and frosty, and even the queen's portrait on the front appeared more unhappy on the five-pound note than on the other banknotes. The ten-pound notes were much nicer, soft and brown and looking as though they had been lying in the sun before arriving in the purse.

The copper coins, the one and two-pence bits, were a bit of a hassle because they were always running in the path of the other coins, tripping them up. After all, the larger coins couldn't see them. There always appeared to be a couple of them in the bag, perhaps because the lady really wanted to use them because she purchased too little.

There were severalfifty-pence bits, but they were only for display because they had straight sides and were the most expensive of the silver coins.

Why are you staring at the one-pound coin? The ten-pence piece was staring at a five-pence piece that was leaning next to it.

The queen on the five-pence piece frowned and fluttered her eyelashes.

Isn't it handsome? said the five-pence coin, so round and sleek and such a lovely colour.

It's no good dressing like that, a pound would never talk to a five-pence, and you're just too bad.

Without responding, the five-pence piece rolled around the purse and gazed adoringly at the pound coin.

The five pence said, "You're so lovely." Is it possible that I'm in love with you?

The pound slowly turned around and looked at the five-pence piece, then at the queen's head in the middle.

What a kooky poppy! The pound coin let out a snort. For coins, the words'silly' and 'poppy' are somewhat derogatory. As a result, the pound coin was twice as bad as the five-pence token.

I'm in lust! The five-pound note smiled and began to chuckle.

HA, HA, HA, HA, HA, HA, HA, HA, HA, HA, HA, The ten-pound note squealed. Stoppit, you're making me laugh so much that I'm curling up in a ball.

The laughter dispersed across the pouch before all of the notes rustled with laughter, and all of the coins tingled with delight.

The five-pence fragment rolled away from the one-pound coin, hurt and angry. The other silver coins, on the other hand, were laughing. The fifty-pence coin chuckled so hard that it fell onto its back, and the ten-penny bits laughed so hard that they rattled against each other.

The five pence fragment flattened itself against the side of the purse and attempted not to be seen until finding a dark spot.

110

ZIIINNNNNGGGGGGGGGGGGGGGGGGGGGGGGGGGGGGGG

GG Both of the coins knelt as a result of the harsh rasping crash. The purse's zipper had been undone. Sunshine spilled into the purse, and all the coins and bills sat motionless, contemplating who would be the one to be wasted.

Instead of the woman's large hand accepting coins and bills, another banknote was placed into the pocket.

ZIIINNNNNGGGGGGGGGGGGGGGGGGGGGGGGGGGGGGGG

GG The purse's zip was yanked shut. The latest banknote drew the attention of the notes and coins. And he looked and stared even more. It wasn't a five-pound bill, a ten-pound bill, or a twenty-pound bill. It was a color they'd never seen before, both crimson and sophisticated.

The wealthiest note in the purse, the twenty-pound note, glared down its queen's nose at the newcomer.

With all the red on you, you look really flashy. It was said in a snobbish tone.

And the queen on the ten-pound note shook her head in mockery.

The red note remained silent.

In reality, you seem to be quite inexpensive! The ten-pound note bent over and brushed up against the red note. And you're very thick. The other notes and coins started to chuckle as well.

And your queen's head is much larger than ours, so you must have a huge head! The five-pound note burst out laughing at its joke, and all the other notes and coins followed suit.

And the copper coins laughed, which was shocking since nothing ever made them chuckle, and the silver coins were bashing on each other with delight.

The five-penny piece in the corner, on the other hand, did not laugh; it understood how rotten it was to see someone looking at it.

What's the deal for everyone's laughter? The five-pence coin broke. You should be courteous and accept the new note. The five-pence item was already very irritated.

The purse was silent. The five-pence piece drew the attention of both the coins and notes. The five-penny coin gulped. Maybe it shouldn't have mentioned that.

You dumb little silver stupidity! The five-pound note screamed, tears flowing down its queen's cheeks. Return to your corner and learn to enjoy yourself!

The whole bag began to shake as the coins helped each other up to keep from falling with laughter.

The five-pence piece rolled back to its corner painfully, nearly buckling in humiliation.

The red note smoothed itself out; it was far larger than the other notes, and some of the coins had to lean against the purse's sides to create space. Many of the wrinkles on the paper gradually disappeared, and the other coins and notes will see the amount on the hand of the large red note.

The twenty-pound note took a gulp. The queen on the ten-pound note closed her doors, and the five-pound note folded up and fell asleep. All of the coins trembled with terror.

Fifty quid! I squinted at a ten-pence slice. It's a fifty-pound bill! A gasp erupted across the purse. They'd heard of fifty-pound bills before, but no one had ever seen one.

They became the most valuable and powerful notes in the country.

I find you're a rotten bunch! The fifty-pound notice rang out. And you are particularly impolite and unpleasant. The large red note approached the twenty-pound note and glared threateningly at its queen's eyes.

There isn't enough space in this purse for all of us.

The frightened twenty-pound note rustled.

Simply fold yourself like a five-pound note and flutter into a corner! The twenty-pound note folded itself once, twice, then three times before disappearing into a shadowy corner of the purse.

The queen on the fifty-pound note then grinned. The five-pence rolled uncomfortably while the fifty-pound note smiled at it.

You were the first person that didn't make fun of me! The huge red note rang out. You also attempted to assist.

The large red note rippled over to the five-pence coin and wrapped softly around it. You're a lovely coin, and you'll be my assistant. I'm going to take care of you!

The five-pence coin trembled along the edges; no one had ever been so kind to it.

As a result, the fifty-pound note and the little five-pence piece become best buds, and if either of the other coins did something naughty to the little five-pence piece, the fifty-pound note would wrap it around until it almost suffocated.

On the other hand, people don't keep fifty-pound notes on them too long in case anyone wants to rob them.

The woman went to a diner one day, and at the end of the meal, she reached into her purse and took out the fifty-pound bill.

ZIIINNNNNGGGGGGGGGGGGGGGGGGGGGGGGGGGGGGGG GG The purse was zip-locked shut. The queen's eyes welled up with tears as she looked at the tiny five-penny item – it had missed its mate.

Although its melancholy was short-lived.

Now, you filthy little scumbag! The twenty-pound note was emerging and advancing towards the little five-pence coin threateningly. Your fifty-pound pal will no longer defend you! "Do you get what that means?"

The terrified tinkling of the five-pence coin.

No, it chirped.

It means I'm going to turn you over every day of the week!

The five-penny piece was about to roll into a corner when...ZIIINNNNNGGG! The bag opened, a hand reached for a handful of coins, and...ZIIINNNNGGG!

The purse was locked once more.

The twenty-pound note blinked, and the five-pence coin had vanished!

I'm leaving a tip because that was such a wonderful meal. The purse's owner put some coins on the fifty-pound notice next to the meal bill.

The queen's eyes brightened when she saw the little five-pence coin was back with its mate!

When the waiter put all of the money in the till, the five-pence piece rolled into the fifty-pound bill, and they cuddled all night.

As the coins returned to the pouch, they realized they had learnt a valuable lesson: good things happen to nice coins, while nasty ones are left in the dark.

What became of the five-pence piece and the fifty-pound note? So, when the restaurant manager brought all the money to the bank, the fifty-pound note and the five-pence slice... But that is a different matter, which I will tell you another day.

The Lovely Princess

Once upon a time, there was a lovely princess. When the sun shone on her blond locks, it glowed so brilliantly that people had to wear shades. When she entered a venue, her skin was so white that people might switch off the lights because she brightened the space so much. Her blue eyes could make you feel calm even on the hottest day.

Her lips glowed in the silence, and her teeth were so bright that her smile dazzled, and people had to put their shades back on.

People stared in wonder as she walked by, and as she spoke, her sentences appeared to tinkle from heaven.

Her father, the King, was extremely proud of his daughter, and when the time came for her to marry, several suitors were willing to marry the princess. Her father, however, turned them all down, believing they were unsuitable for his daughter.

Then there was a BOOM!

The arrival of Prince William

Where the princess was lovely, he was dashing. He was, in truth, the most beautiful prince, the princess and her father had ever seen.

He was as big as a ruby post and as straight as a ruby post. His hair was as dark as tar and curled tightly over his brow. In reality, it was so dark that when the sun came up, people had to remove their sunglasses. His complexion was flawless and so sun-tanned that his olive body gleamed in the candlelight. His eyes were green and sparkled like emeralds, and his teeth shone as he grinned, and his face was still filled with laughter.

So it was revealed that the prince and princess would marry the following April, much to the delight and satisfaction of all the people of the kingdom.

The following day, the prince welcomed the princess on a cruise across the capital's bay to see her city from the water.

The prince's boat was tiny, and the tide was high, so the boat was quickly washed out to sea.

C'MON! Exclaimed the prince to his oarsmen. Put the heart and soul through it.

Regardless of how well the oarsmen worked, and still with the prince and princess on board, their boat was eventually washed out to sea.

Hello there! The prince had noticed another ship from his telescope and was requesting assistance from it.

The other boats, much larger than the princes and equipped with massive sails, approached the prince's ships.

The prince's joy at being rescued abruptly dissipated. To his surprise, when the huge boat approached, the prince saw a flag at the peak of the middle mast. A black banner, a black flag with a white skull and crossbones in the middle!

A pirate ship's banner!

Brown Beard was bent over the edge, laughing at them! The sea's most hated pirate!

HA, HA, HA! He yelled. YOU'VE HAS BEEN WARNED!

The pirate ship swayed violently while the pirate team delighted in dancing about. They'd kidnapped a prince and a bride!

Brown Beard was a terrifying figure. With a cruel face that hurt Brown Beard to carry. He never wanted shades, except in the brightest sunlight, because his eyes were too dark. When he approached, he seemed like a huge black crab charging at you, and when he screamed, which he always did, filthy rotting teeth behind thin, lifeless lips made his inhuman face much more menacing.

His dark beard was long and worn, and it was a mess because he kept treading on it.

But the most frightening sight of all was crouched on his shoulder: a massive black and hooded scavenger. What a vulture!

The prince drew his princess close behind him.

You'll never be able to take us alive! He yelled as he waved his sword.

Brown Beard snarled, "I don't believe you have a preference."

A net was thrown down from the pirate ship onto the prince and princess and then hauled back up with the prince and princess struggling inside at the pirate's warning.

Brown Beard's normal scowl was replaced with a triumphant grin for the first time since Christmas.

Take them to the bilge! He burst out laughing.

The bilge on a ship is a horrible place; it is at the bottom of the boat, where all the polluted water and garbage are dumped. It's dark and damp, and it feels like all you can think about.

Don't worry; the Prince reassured the Princess. We're going to flee!

Brown Beard burst out laughing as he learned this.

Nobody ever leaves my bilge,' he screamed. Just when they've died! " The hatch slammed down. The princess looked terrified as she held the prince's hand in hers.

On the castle's terrace, the King awaited the prince and princess. He set up a table with plates of doughnuts, chocolate sandwiches, and sparkling water because he figured the princess would like all of them.

Instead of the prince's sweet little boat returning, the bay was covered with the large black shadow of the pirate ship.

The pirate ship did not frighten the King; he had plenty of huge guns in the castle that could easily destroy it. But he was taken aback when he saw the prince's tiny boat crossing from the pirate ship to the castle harbour.

The pirate who escaped was a shambles; in reality, he was such a shambles that the King nearly kicked him into the sea.

He wore an eye patch above his ear because he lacked an ear patch. He'd cut the toes off his large leather pirate boots because they pinched his toes, and he'd never used his dagger because he'd forgotten the handle!

But when the pirate handed him Brown Beard's message, the King forgot all about it. His eyes widened with terror.

A CHEST FILLED WITH GOLD!

Brown beard demanded a chest full of gold in gratitude for the prince and princess's return.

That was all the gold the King possessed. Yet his excitement at regaining custody of the Prince and Princess was indescribable. He planned a lavish banquet complete with trumpeters, clowns, a DJ, and still more doughnuts.

The prince was enraged.

I was going to flee! He yelled. And return your princess.

The King made a shaky motion of his head.

What are you doing on a cruise in the middle of the ocean? The King grinned. It's impossible!

But... The prince looked around at the banquet and all the visitors, thinking, "If you've offered the pirate all your gold, you can't manage all of this; you must now be bad."

The King grinned.

True, I'll be broke at Christmas.

All in the banqueting hall was staring at the King. What was he on about?

The gold coins I gave the pirate were really chocolate coins wrapped in gold foil that I planned to send as Christmas gifts! The king chuckled. I do have all of my genuine gold!

And if the pirate's boat was a long way out at sea, they could both hear the frustration cries.

When the pirate opened the chest of gold coins and saw them gleaming in the light, his eyes popped out with rage as they melted and steadily rolled onto the ground!

CPSIA information can be obtained
at www.ICGtesting.com
Printed in the USA
BVHW091716180621
609900BV00004B/1133